THE PUBLIC IN YOUR WOODS

ɔre f.

sta..f   contact

eek Lc

?-3 FE

THE PUBLIC IN YOUR WOODS

*An owner's guide to managing
urban-fringe woodland for recreation*

J. A. Irving

A LAND DECADE EDUCATIONAL COUNCIL PUBLICATION

PACKARD PUBLISHING LIMITED
CHICHESTER

First published in 1985 by
Packard Publishing Limited, 16 Lynch Down,
Funtington, Chichester, West Sussex PO18 9LR

ISBN 0 906527 19 8

Typeset by Pauline Newton, Chichester, West Sussex
Additional artwork by Bruce Williams Designs, Bosham, West Sussex
Printed in the United Kingdom by Chanctonbury Press Limited,
West Chiltington, Sussex

TABLE OF CONTENTS

Table of Contents continued . . .

Table of Contents continued . . .

Table of Contents continued . . .

PART III

Table of Contents continued . . .

List of Tables

Table of Contents continued . . .

List of Plates

Table of Contents continued . . .

ACKNOWLEDGEMENTS

This book has been prepared for the Land Decade Educational Council, as part of a two-year research fellowship funded by the Ernest Cook Trust and the Radcliffe Trust. The Department of Geography, University College London, provided the office accommodation and technical services. The author is particularly grateful for the advice, help and encouragement given by the Council's Fellowship Advisory Committee, chaired by Graham Moss (Land Council) and whose members included Dr D M Harding, Dr C M Harrison, Dr A Warren, Col D A Campbell, Mrs M Laverack, and Dr J Peachey. Further, without the information so freely provided by woodland managers and others involved with forestry and recreation, this book could not have been written.

J. A. Irving

PREFACE

Who shall use the land? and How shall the land be used? are time-less questions, for, in the last analysis, land is the resource of which the supply is permanently finite. When the Land Decade Educational Council was established as a charity for education and research in 1979 we were deeply conscious that in Britain, and particularly in the more populated parts of it, that finite quantity of *rural* land was diminishing at a rate which gave rise for concern as it was converted to urban and sub-urban uses, while derelict urban land was allowed to lie wasted.

It has been said that every town-dwelling Englishman is a countryman at heart. While nowadays this is a manifest exaggeration it is true that, given the chance, in their leisure time a large number of town-dwellers enjoy nothing better than to visit the countryside; countryside upon which the pressures are many — farming and forestry, conservation of wildlife or scenery, quiet recreation and organized leisure. The pressures are particularly high on the fringes of towns themselves, where, unless great care is exercised, a particular kind of rural degeneration can occur. Well-managed woodland close to urban areas has above all other land a capacity to absorb large numbers both of people and of activities, yet no handbook for woodland owners, recreation managers, or local authority staff, has been readily available. To fill this gap, and at the same time to share the collective knowledge on the subject the Land Decade Council, with assistance from the Radcliffe and Ernest Cook Trusts, commissioned Mr Irving to research and write this book.

Ralph Verney
January 1985

SUMMARY

This book is about coping with increased access in your woodlands. It does not call for more access, rather it takes a pragmatic view of woodland recreation and the underlying theory is this: planned provision for increased public use is far better than belated attempts to control *de facto* access.

The book concentrates on woodland in the urban fringe, which is the current 'front line' where owners face most problems. It will also be of use to land owners in more rural areas who also face demands for access, or wish to consider recreational enterprises. The book is in three parts.

Part I sketches the potential of woodland for recreation, how it is used now, and how it could be used more imaginatively. Part II shows how to assess the potential of your woodland, how in practical terms to cope with increased public access, and what strategies and management techniques to adopt. Part III contains appendices, showing who can help with advice, detailed designs, labour and financial support. The key points of the book are listed below.

- Woodland has a special character as a recreation area by virtue of its stature, screening, shelter and longevity, which are particularly valuable as a contrast to the urban environment (Chapter 2).
- The principal recreation resources of a woodland are the open areas, glades, rides and paths, whereas the stands of trees act only as a scenic backcloth for most recreation (Chapter 2).
- The urban fringe is used for recreation more like town parks. Visits are regular, short in duration and a wide range of social groups is represented (Chapter 3).
- The common activities in urban fringe woodlands are, in order of decreasing popularity, walking, picnicking, dog walking, children playing, horse riding, jogging and naturalist pursuits (Chapter 3).
- Activities which have great potential in urban fringe woodlands include play areas, barbecue sites, off-road cycling, BMX cycling, trim trails, wayfaring, camping and caravan sites, provision for the elderly or disabled, a restaurant, chalets and hostels, educational use for schools and the public, and community involvement in management (Chapters 4, 5 and 6).

- The potential of a woodland is principally affected by access, local population, soil type, area and shape, open areas, woodland type and hazards (Chapter 7).
- A series of levels of management are described ranging from minimum, such as leasing, to total owner-involvement as the developer of major facilities (Chapter 8).
- A key element in site management is contact with the public, many of whom are regular visitors and can help with patrolling (Chapter 8).
- Of the impact that recreation can have on a woodland, horse trampling is the most serious, whereas disturbance to wildlife and fire hazard are surprisingly less significant (Chapter 9).
- Recreation can be readily accommodated within most commercial woodlands as it imposes few operating constraints in addition to those already encountered in an urban fringe location (Chapter 10).
- Of the activities common in urban fringe woodland, riding is the least compatible with other pursuits and needs to be segregated (Chapter 11).

The most significant subject in the book is public education, or 'interpretation'. Through interpretation landowners can transmit something of their enthusiasm and feelings for woodland and thereby nurture over a period of years a symapthetic attitude in their visitors (Chapters 5 and 6).

A recreation plan check-list is given in Table 7.5 at the end of Chapter 7.

1. WHY OPEN YOUR WOODLAND?

1.1 Who is providing for woodland recreation?

Traditionally woodland recreation has been provided mainly by the Forestry Commission and to a much lesser extent by local authorities, whereas the private woodland owner has rarely encouraged public access or provided facilities. Forestry Commission holdings are mostly in the uplands away from centres of population, whereas much of the woodland near towns is in private or occasionally in local authority ownership.

1.2 What are the trends in demand?

Recent trends in outdoor recreation show that 60 per cent of trips are to destinations within 3 km of the edge of towns (the 'urban fringe'), and it seems likely that demand will increase in this area [1]. The growth of interest in fitness, the BMX-bike craze, and the growing demand for riding are examples of the recreation pressures now exerted on the urban fringe. The current slow-down in economic growth is also affecting recreation as activities closer to town become more attractive than longer trips. Woodlands near housing are well placed to make an important contribution to society as recreation areas, particularly for people without personal transport and others less fortunate. As a result of these trends, the urban fringe and its woodland is facing a demand for public access and recreation greater than ever before.

1.3 The challenge of increasing political pressure

Until recently groups calling for increased access have been mainly concerned with the countryside, but their attention is now turning to the urban fringe. Concern about the lack of response by the private sector to these demands for access is being expressed by pressure groups such as the Ramblers' Association which recently called for Access Agreements or Orders to private woodland in the urban fringe [2]. Such demands for access legislation may be widely supported in Parliament now that so few Members are experienced in rural land management, let alone forestry, but as Kenneth Royston has pointed out, this is not the solution [3].

[1] Numbers in square brackets denote references which are given on page 146.

1.4 How can landowners respond to such demands for access?

Mr Royston who is land agent on the Duke of Buccleuch's Boughton Estate just outside Kettering, calls on owners to be more public relations-minded, to meet the access problems halfway, to explore how more facilities can be provided for visitors, and to educate the public about life in the countryside. The reasoning of this argument is simple: planned provision of access, compatible with woodland and estate management, is in the interests of both the public and the landowner. This approach is clearly preferable to an enforced access order, or belated recognition of *de facto* access in an inappropriate location. For its efforts to bridge the gap between urban and rural communities, the Boughton Estate received the 1983 Countryside Commission/Country Landowners' Association Award, and is described in Chapter 6.

1.5 Public education is essential

Public education about estate management, and especially forest management is essential for increased access, if the woodland is to be appreciated and conflict with other land uses minimized. There is great ignorance among the general public about forestry methods and objectives, which is not dispelled by the long time-scale of woodland management and periods of apparent inactivity. Fortunately, however, one of the current growth areas of public interest is in all aspects of rural life, local history and country crafts. Forestry can be used to illustrate all three of these themes and the woodland owner has a great opportunity to explain forestry to the public. In the urban fringe this opportunity is enhanced by the wider range of social groups in the potential audience, unlike countryside recreation where the car-driving, middle-class people predominate.

1.6 Coping with increased access

Landowners are now accepting that the demand for increased access is best met with planned provision, rather than with belated recognition. The Country Landowners' Association has recognized access as a key issue requiring a positive response and recently has produced a booklet for members giving guidance, entitled *Agreeing on Access* [4]. The Timber Growers are also aware of the demand for access to woodland and are to publish a code of practice in 1985.

As a contribution to solving the practical problems that increased access brings, the Land Decade Educational Council sponsored this book which aims to provide the owner with guidance on assessing a woodland's potential for recreation, the management techniques and strategies applicable, and sources of funds, advice and assistance. This book also hopes to reassure landowners and woodland managers that coping with increased access and other urban fringe pressures, is no more difficult than the other forest management problems they face. Most forms of recreation are not great money spinners, but support from grants, manpower and tax relief can help reduce the burden. However, by providing for access on a planned basis, the landowner has the opportunity to foster a sympathetic public, which is a wise investment over the longer term, as demand for access increases and new activities appear.

1.7 The scope of the book

This book looks forward to how woodlands can be used in the future. For example, can foresters and landowners capture the imagination of both school children and the wider public, to communicate something of their enthusiasm and feeling for trees and woodlands? Are there certain groups of people who are not catered for with the existing styles of facilities and site layout, for example the elderly or infirm and disabled? Can woodlands be made more fun for both children and adults? Can visitors be given a broader experience of woodland?

The material on which this book is based has been gathered from the literature, site surveys, and discussions with woodland managers and others involved with forestry and recreation.

The guide concentrates on the urban fringe as current trends indicate that woodland in this area is facing the greatest demands for access and experiencing the most pressing problems of dumping, trespass and vandalism. Despite this focus on the urban fringe, the book will also be useful to woodland owners in more rural areas, who face demands for increased access or wish to consider recreational enterprises.

1.8 The structure of the book

This book is in three parts. Part I looks at what woodland can offer, how it is used now, the developing trends in use, and how it could be used more imaginatively. Part II shows in practical terms how to open your woodland to the public, how to assess its potential, and the management strategies and techniques involved. Part III contains appendices showing who can help with sources of detailed designs, advice, labour and funding.

2. WHAT ARE THE OPPORTUNITIES FOR WOODLAND RECREATION?

2.1 The special character of woodland

There are certain features of woodland, which although very familiar to a forester, set it apart as a rather special environment for the visitor. These features are: stature, shelter, screening and age. Trees are the only form of life larger than mankind that are encountered every day. Their height, breadth, complexity of form and myriad component parts are a very strong reminder of the natural world. The sheer size of trees, particularly when grouped together in woodland, can impress even the least sensitive visitor. It is the stature of trees which can give the visitor an immediate sense of the presence of nature.

Partly as a result of their size, trees modify conditions beneath the canopy or in adjacent open areas, providing shelter and shade for visitors. The variable light intensity within woodland, the patterns of dappled shade and the contrast between sunny rides and shady groves are an ever-changing source of visual interest (Plate 1). During wet and windy weather visitors are more attracted to woodland than open parks, and on very hot days woods provide refreshing coolness and shade. In and around towns the capacity of trees to absorb noise, dust and carbon dioxide is especially beneficial both to visitors and nearby residents. Shelter is sometimes a disadvantage for the woodland manager as the higher humidity and cooler temperatures prevent wet rides and paths drying out quickly. This is discussed further in Chapter 9.

The screening effect of a woodland is one of its most valuable features for recreation. On entering a wood the visitor soon can be isolated from the surrounding landscape, and also from other visitors which relieves the feeling of over-crowding. This gives woodland a high capacity to absorb visitors and yet provide them with a sense of nature and peace. Screening has important

Plate 1 — The patterns of dappled shade and the contrast between sunny rides and shady groves.

implications for visitor management, as without visible landmarks visitors have difficulty in finding their way around, unless they are 'regulars'. Whilst there is a sense of adventure in exploring a wood for the first time, which can be particularly important for children, this uncertainty can deter many adults from straying away from the car park, or main entrance. Screening also provides an ingredient of surprise on a woodland visit; who knows what view or wildlife may be round the next corner.

The fourth aspect of woodland is its age and apparent permanence in the landscape. Local residents and visitors alike appreciate the apparent timeless quality of woodland and its permanence in a landscape which is otherwise continually changing [5]. This long time-scale in relation to our life-span, the comparatively long periods between forest operations and the widespread ignorance of forestry methods often results in misconceptions of woodland as a static feature. These attitudes have silvicultural implications for amenity woodland, favouring systems which retain tree cover, like group selection or coppicing small areas, rather than wholesale clearfelling (see Chapter 10).

Woodland, therefore, is rather special by providing visitors with a strong impression of nature, sheltering them from the weather, noise and dirt of the nearby town, screening them from the outside world and their fellows and giving them a sense of timelessness in an ever-changing world. It is this natural atmosphere, peace, quiet and seclusion which attracts most woodland visitors [6]. The value of this experience is greatest in areas where the surrounding landscape is most urban or industrial, and it is therefore these woodlands close to town which have much to offer visitors.

2.2 What parts of a woodland are used for recreation?

Except in mature woodland with no undergrowth like beech woods, most visitors keep to paths, rides, glades and other open areas which may adjoin or lie within the woodland. It is these rides and open areas which are a woodland's true recreation resource, where most activities occur (Plate 2). The stands of trees act more as the backcloth or scenic framework against which the activities take place. The fact that visitors stay on the rides and in the open areas means they are in effect confined to a very small part of the total area of the site. Their limited pene-

Plate 2 — The recreation value of woodland principally lies in its open areas, glades and rides.

tration of the stands and plantations results in highly localized fire hazards and limited disturbance of wildlife. The implications of this are discussed further in Chapter 9.

There are several exceptions to this general rule where visitors do penetrate the stands and plantations: children playing, naturalists, orienteers and dogs. In woodlands near towns, particularly those close to housing which can act as play areas for the local children, the plantations and stands will be subject to most use and disturbance. Naturalists and orienteers are relatively uncommon visitors and both types are generally aware of the sensitive woodland environment they are using. Dogs off the lead roam the plantations following their noses and are common in the urban fringe.

2.3 What recreational needs can a woodland meet?

Human needs for recreation cover a wide range from spiritual refreshment and aesthetic appreciation to exercise and overnight

accommodation. Table 2.1 lists some recreational needs and
divides them into four groups dealing with physical welfare,
social contact, escapism and mental stimulation. None of these
needs is met by one specific activity and most are met by a wide
variety of pursuits. Table 2.1 also gives examples of activities
which can meet each of the needs for recreation.

Table 2.1 — Recreational needs and woodland activities

Physical welfare

Overnight accommodation	Camping, caravanning
Eating and drinking	Picnicking, barbecues
Exercise	Jogging, cycling

Social contact

Companionship	Family walk, group camping
Competition	Orienteering, archery
Community involvement	Voluntary wardening, meeting friends

Escapism

Relaxation	Playing, resting
Solitude	Walking, wildlife observation
Peace	Walking at dusk or dawn
Spiritual refreshment	Walking, wildlife observation
Clean air	Cycling, camping
Experiencing natural environment	Walking, picking fruit or fungi
Freedom from responsibilities	Camping, jogging

Mental stimulation

Aesthetic appreciation	Photography, painting
Sense of continuity	Periodic visits, local history studies
Creating something	Voluntary site management
Entertainment	BMX cycling, playing
Excitement	Shooting, orienteering
Novel experience	Wildlife observation, exploring
Learning/improving a skill	Riding, understanding nature

Obviously any one activity is able to meet a variety of needs simultaneously; riding can meet the needs for exercise, companionship, relaxation, entertainment and improving a skill. An early morning walk with the dog can meet the needs for exercise, relaxation, solitude, peace, spiritual refreshment and over a period of years, a sense of continuity. All the examples of activities listed in Table 2.1 can take place in woodland, which indicates the great potential this environment has for meeting needs for recreation. But how is woodland in the urban fringe actually used?

3. HOW ARE WOODLANDS USED TODAY?

3.1 How popular is woodland for recreation?

The brief answer is, 'not very'. In a major survey of Scottish residents by Edinburgh University only 18 per cent of people interviewed had made trips to woodland in the previous twelve months [7]. A study of an urban wood in Sheffield found a similar figure, only 21 per cent of people interviewed used the wood on a regular basis, but a further 26 per cent had used the wood in the past [5]. The minority appeal of woodland is very obvious at places with both woodland and grassland, as the open space attracts the majority and only a minority seek the peace and naturalness of woodland [6,7]. Elsewhere, particularly woodland near housing which suffers from a lack of alternative parks or open spaces nearby, the woodland can be locally important, but such instances are uncommon. The secondary attraction of woodland in relation to open areas becomes very important when considering the recreation potential of a woodland, as its recreational value principally lies in its open areas, glades and rides, see Table 3.1. Few activities use the woodland stands and plantations.

3.2 Are there specific woodland activities?

Most activities are not specific to woodlands and can easily take place elsewhere, but a large number of activities are possible in woodlands. A team from Reading University assessed the site requirements of each activity listed in Table 3.1 [8,9]. While all these are feasible in woodland only five really depend on a wood-

Table 3.1 — Activities feasible in woodland and main use areas

Activity	Open Areas	Glades	Rides	Stands
Informal activities				
Children playing	**	**	*	**
Cycling			**	
Dog walking	*	*	**	*
Horse riding			**	
Jogging			**	
Nut, fruit, fungi picking	*	**	**	
Picnicking	**	**	*	
Sightseeing	*	*	*	
Cross-country skiing	**			
Trail-bike riding		*	**	
Walking	*	*	**	
Wayfaring	**	**	**	**
Wildlife observation†	**	**	**	*
Overnight activities				
Camping	**	**		
Caravanning	**	**		
Chalets/hostels	**			
Field sports				
Archery	**	**	**	
Clay-pidgeon shooting	**			
Full-bore shooting	**			
Small-bore shooting	**			
Pheasant shooting	**	**	**	
Deer shooting		**	**	
Rough shooting	**	**	**	
Hunting foxes, deer	**	**	**	
Competitive sports				
Cyclocross	**	**	**	
Golf	**			
Modern pentathlon	**			
Motor-car sports			**	
Motor-cycle sports			**	
Orienteering	**	**	**	**

** Main use
 * Minor use
 † Throughout this book wildlife observation is used to cover all naturalist pursuits

land setting. These are collecting nuts, fruit or fungi, orienteering and its non-competitive form wayfaring, field archery and deer shooting. In woodlands with extensive water features, such as ponds, lakes and rivers, the range of activities can be extended further to include water sports such as fishing and swimming. Water sports are considered to be peripheral to the subject of this book, and are not discussed further. From the long list of pursuits in Table 3.1, the most common in woodland are the informal activities, particularly walking, picnicking, sightseeing and wildlife observation.

3.3 Are the activities different in urban fringe woodlands?

Yes, in the urban fringe, the range of activities is narrower, the most common being:

> Children playing
> Dog walking
> Horse riding
> Jogging
> Wildlife observation
> Picnicking
> Walking

This range of activities reflects the special significance of the woodland close to town; it is nearer the centres of population and can be used for more frequent, shorter visits such as dog-walking and jogging. The urban fringe in many places has a high population of horses, and where woodland is connected to the bridlepath network, riding is popular. Where woodland adjoins housing it often acts as the local adventure play-area for children to use without parental supervision, unlike family visits to the countryside.

3.4 How are urban-fringe woodlands used?

Recent surveys [10,11] show that recreation areas in the urban fringe attract visitors from surprisingly small catchment areas, so the local population characteristics, such as its age structure, affluence, or mobility will be crucial influences on the way a woodland is used. Woodlands some distance from the urban areas and ill-served by public transport are only used by the mobile and more affluent sections of the community. By contrast, sites within easy walking-distance of housing (2 km) will attract a broader section of the community, not just the more affluent car-owners. In this way a woodland within walking distance of housing will be used as a local park for nearby residents and would only attract people from a wider area if it has special features like a barbecue area, or autumn colours. The 2 km easy walking-distance seems to be a critical factor determining the use of a woodland, as those sites further than 2 km from any centre of population will draw mainly on motorized visitors and horse-riders.

Woodland close to urban areas can be used for short visits, or unplanned trips to take advantage of a break in bad weather. The most significant result is that most visitors become *regular* users of the site. The proportion of regular visitors is highest near the urban areas and decreases further away from town. Regular visitors have important management implications; they know the site so do not require directional signs, and they may act as additional eyes and ears for the manager by reporting problems or interesting events.

3.5 How do woodland activities vary through time?

Informal activities in urban-fringe sites show more constant use through the seasons than sites in more rural locations, although winter attendance is lower than summer [11]. In the spring and autumn when the weather is less predictable, making visits closer to home more attractive, some urban-fringe sites are busier than in summer. At such times the shelter or the seasonal attractions of spring flowers and autumn colours can draw more visitors to woodlands than more open parks (Plate 3).

The pattern of use through the week also varies with the proximity to urban development. The further a wood is from the urban area, the more the weekend dominates the weekly attendance figures. This reflects the visitor's need to plan trips to more distant locations, whereas a visit to the local park can be spontaneous or make use of shorter periods of free time. Queen Elizabeth Country Park, a wooded park on the South Downs 18 km north of Portsmouth, receives half its weekly attendance on Sunday, whereas at Cathkin Braes on Glasgow's urban fringe the Sunday proportion is only a quarter of the weekly use.

Weekday attendance begins with dog walkers, joggers and people on their way to work or school if the woodland is well connected to the local path system or offers a convenient short cut.

Plate 3 — The seasonal attractions of spring flowers.

Plate 4 — Visitors passing through Linford Wood, Milton Keynes, on the New Town pedestrian system.

Linford Wood in Milton Keynes for example (Plate 4) is linked to
the New Town pedestrian system and about one-fifth of its visitors
just pass through [12,13]. At lunchtime woodland car parks are
popular with working people having sandwiches in the car and
woodlands near industry are often used for lunchtime jogging,
e.g., Brazenose Wood near BL's Cowley plant. Afternoons are
generally busier than mornings with more dog walkers, walkers,
the occasional horse rider, and school children returning home or
playing after school. Early evening brings the final wave of joggers,
dog walkers and walkers, then at dusk a woodland car park will be
used for courting.

Weekends bring out the horse riders, the weekly walkers, more
children playing and most picnickers. As with weekdays, Saturday
and Sunday mornings are relatively quiet, but busier than weekday
mornings. Weekend afternoons are the busiest, especially Sunday
when attendance reaches a peak about 4 p.m., then declines to a
low level in the early evening.

3.6 How popular are the urban-fringe activities?

The relative importance of these urban-fringe activities obviously
varies with the circumstances of a particular wood. An indication
of the relative popularity of the seven main urban-fringe activities
can be gained by considering the number of daily participants, the
frequency and season of participation, as shown in Table 3.2. The
numbers attending depend on the situation of each woodland, but
an order of magnitude is given to cover sites ranging from small
25-ha woods to larger 100-ha sites with extensive open areas. Of
the seven main activities, walking stands out as being the most
common. Whether a woodland is the focus of the walk or part of
a longer route depends on the extent of its footpath network, but
walking trips in the urban fringe are generally short (under 7 km),
and are accommodated within many sites. Despite being less
popular than walking, dog walking is significant in the urban fringe
because of the regularity of trips pet owners make to exercise
their animals.

Picnicking is only significant at sites with extensive open areas
or glades, and seems least popular in woodlands closest to the
urban areas [10,11,13]. At others with open areas and nearer the
countryside, picnickers dominate the attendance figures for the
summer months, especially at weekends and during the school

Table 3.2 — Relative popularity of urban-fringe activities

Activity	Daily nos.	Frequency	Season
Walking	100s—1000s	Daily—Weekly	Year round + Summer peak
Picnicking	100s—1000s	Weekly	Summer season
Dog walking	10s—100s	Daily—Weekly	Year round
Children playing	10s—100s	Daily—Weekly	Year round + holiday peak
Horse riding	10s—100s	Weekly	Year round
Jogging	10s	Daily—Weekly	Year round
Wildlife observation	10s	Weekly	Year round + Summer peak

holidays. Woodlands with special attractions such as barbecue areas or water features draw large numbers of picnickers, to whom the woodland is merely a scenic backdrop.

Children playing are particularly numerous in woodlands close to the urban areas, where, depending on the density of the undergrowth, they utilize the whole wood not just the rides and glades like most visitors. These woods near housing are used often on a daily if not weekly basis, unlike less frequent family outings to more rural destinations which may give an opportunity for woodland play once a month or less. Thus the popularity of a woodland for children's play will depend on the children living within walking distance, and secondly the children that accompany parents on family visits. At sites with large open areas, the children in family parties may be numerically greater, but it is local children playing without supervision who often have the greater environmental impact as discussed in Chapter 9.

Riding is a minority use and one which rarely uses a woodland as its main focus, unlike walking. Woodland is far more often part of a longer ride through the urban fringe and the degree of use depends very much on the connections between the woodland and the bridleway network outside. Woodland not connected to the bridleway system, surrounded by main roads and away from equestrian centres, for example Oxleas Wood in south-east London, does not attract much riding. While riders are a small minority in comparison with other visitors, their potential for conflict with others and the environmental impact of riding are very significant, and are discussed in Chapters 9 and 11.

Jogging is a recent development of particular significance in the urban fringe and woodland is favoured by joggers as it offers interesting and varied routes. Although most common in woodland near housing areas or industry, even woodland in rural locations is now being used for jogging, for example, Wyre Forest, 10 km west of Kidderminster. The number of joggers in comparison to other visitors is very low in most urban-fringe woodlands, except where special facilities may attract more use, like a trim or fitness trail, or at a series of exercise stations such as a straddle jump bench (Plate 5). Linford Wood in Milton Keynes experienced an increase in joggers from virtually none to around a fifth of regular visitors as a result of installing a trim trail [12,13].

Plate 5 — A straddle jump bench to exercise the legs by jumping zig-zag across the bench.

Wildlife observation is another minority pursuit which draws a small number of regular visitors to urban-fringe woodland. Many visitors indulge in more than one activity when visiting woodland, and wildlife observation is most commonly cited as a secondary reason for visiting woodland [11]. Keen wildlife observers will not stay on the paths and in open areas, but will use the whole woodland as do children playing, but unlike children they do not have significant environmental impact.

As with wildlife observation, some activities are combined with others on a trip, such as a picnic and children playing, or walking the dog and observing wildlife. In the urban fringe, however, activities pursued in isolation are more the norm; children playing without parental supervision, jogging, riding and walking are not often combined with other activities [11]. These urban-fringe activities do not generate litter, as they are often short in duration and not associated with eating, so urban-fringe woodlands without picnic areas are generally very clean. (Dumping domestic refuse may be a greater problem in urban-fringe woodland than litter from visitors; see Chapters 8 and 9.)

3.7 What are the less common activities?

A number of less common activities are associated with urban-fringe woodland and these are listed below. They depend on either the provision of special facilities such as barbecue grills, or localized demand like tourist camping, or a combination of the two. Despite being less common or even rare, these activities are significant because in some instances such as camping they can provide income, unlike most informal use. Secondly, they may also indicate potential growth areas as new activities catch the public interest. A brief comment on the current popularity of these minor activities in urban-fringe woodland is given below, grouped under four headings: informal activities, overnight activities, field sports and competitive sports.

Informal activities

Play areas. These are rarely provided at present, but prove very popular once installed.

Barbecue sites. These are rare and confined to more rural sites but are very well used.

Cycling: BMX. These children's stunt bikes mainly use special competitive tracks but informal use of rough terrain is growing in popularity especially near housing areas.

Cycling: off-road. This is rare but likely to grow; only requires smooth rides or bridlepaths as circuits or part of a larger network.

Nut, fruit and fungi gathering. This is very local and very brief in duration; depends on the extent of the 'crop'.

Trail-bike riding. Widespread in low numbers, mainly by under-age unlicensed riders, who use rough terrain in unfrequented areas.

Trim trail. These are rarely provided at present, but are popular once installed.

Wayfaring. Provision for this non-competitive form of orienteering is uncommon, and rather underused at present.

Overnight activities

Camping. Provision is rare, and confined to special groups such as Scouts, or to tourist areas, but very well used.

Caravanning. Provision is rare and confined to tourist areas but very well used.

Chalets, cabins. Provision is rare, mainly by the Forestry Commission, and confined to tourist areas, but very well used.

Field sports

Field archery. Very rarely provided and is confined to use by clubs.

Pheasant shooting. Very rare in the urban fringe and is limited to more rural areas, where most use is confined to syndicate members.

Rough shooting. Rare, limited to more rural areas and its use is very restricted.

Competitive sports

Orienteering. Provision is growing but the use of particular sites is occasional as the sport demands unfamiliar terrain.

3.8 What is the current role of urban-fringe woodland?

To summarize; the pattern of use in urban-fringe woodlands that emerges is: woodlands are not very popular when compared with other recreation sites, and most activities are not specific to woodlands. There are seven pursuits common to urban fringe woods:

Walking	Widespread, significant in large numbers;
Picnicking	Locally significant in large numbers;
Dog walking	Widespread, significant but moderate numbers;
Children playing	Locally significant, but moderate numbers;
Horse riding	Locally significant, but low numbers;
Jogging	Widespread, in very low numbers;
Wildlife observation	Widespread, in very low numbers.

Woodlands in the urban fringe have small catchment areas and sites within 2 km of housing will attract a significant proportion of visitors on foot. Regular visitors are most numerous at sites nearest housing, and decrease with distance away from town. Urban-fringe woodland attracts visitors throughout the year, and may be busiest in spring and autumn rather than the summer peak associated with non-wooded recreational sites.

The nearer a woodland is to the urban area, the more even the spread of visitors will be through the week and the less dominant the Sunday attendance figures. Weekday mornings are the most quiet periods, with more visitors in the afternoons. At weekends attendance is higher and Sunday afternoon is the busiest period.

The urban-fringe woodland clearly has two roles. First, it provides a widespread local resource for exercise and play for the seven common informal activities and the rarer informal variants listed in 3.7. This role of acting as a base for informal activities is currently the most significant function for urban-fringe woodland. Its secondary role is to act as a resource for the more specialist pursuits like overnight activities, field sports and orienteering, which are very restricted in their distribution, but are significant for the private owner as they offer more opportunities for income than is generally the case for informal activities. But how could urban-fringe woodland be used in the future, and with more imagination? These are the subjects of the next two chapters.

4. MEETING THE TRENDS IN WOODLAND ACTIVITIES

4.1 What are the underlying social trends?

While the current slow rate of economic growth and high level of unemployment persists, the demand for recreation in the urban fringe is likely to increase at the expense of visits further afield. When money is short people favour locations nearer home for walks and family picnics [1]. As the economy recovers the reverse trend may well occur as picnickers and walkers on day trips return to more distant locations using the sites nearer home only for local exercise and play.

Due to a greater proportion of the population reaching retirement age, coupled with more redundancy and early retirement, the number of retired people is increasing. This group is likely to place increased demand on urban-fringe sites and is able to visit woodlands at off-peak times when the rest of the population is working or at school. Retired people and the younger middle-aged are showing great interest in the environment, particularly local history, country crafts and natural history [1]. Here is an opportunity for the woodland owner to explain woodland crafts, silvicultural methods, and the problems of the long time-scale for woodland management, which is discussed more fully in Chapter 5.

More young married couples are delaying having children and therefore have more free time [1]. When this is coupled with the growing awareness of keeping fit and taking regular exercise, it will place greater demand on all kinds of sports facilities. This demand is particularly relevant to jogging and trim trails which are well suited to urban-fringe woodland. Off-road cycling, wayfaring and orienteering also may increase in popularity as a result of the interest in fitness.

There is also political pressure for greater access to private land, including woodland. User organizations such as the Ramblers' Association are calling for Access Agreements or Access Orders to private woodland in the urban fringe, under the provisions of the 1968 *Countryside Act* [2,14]. Some pressure groups consider a right of public access to private woodland is inevitable in the not too distant future [4]. Such political pressure when combined with the growth in demand for urban-fringe recreation could result in Access Orders being implemented.

4.2 How can this rising demand be met?

The simplest approach is to permit access to the woodland but not provide any special facilities, like picnic tables, and restrict any activities which the landowner considers to be incompatible with the objectives and circumstances of the woodland. An example of this approach, Hockeridge Wood in Hertfordshire, is described in Chapter 6. The seven common activities listed in Table 4.1 below are most likely to be the first to show the rise in demand and these can be accommodated in woodland relatively easily as shown in the table. It is important to emphasize that walking, jogging and wildlife observation are the most suited to woodland, and the others all may have one or more disadvantages, the most problematic being horse riding. These disadvantages may or may not be significant for an owner, according to his objectives and the circumstances of his woodland. These problems of environmental impact, conflict with forestry and with other recreation activities are given detailed consideration in Part II of this book, which also includes how to assess the potential of your woodland. Part III of the book contains appendices which give sources of technical advice, labour and grants.

Table 4.1 — Suitability of the common activities to woodland

Walking:	Environmental impact low; no conflict with other activities, no facilities required.
Picnicking:	Litter can be a problem, no conflict with other activities, car access preferable.
Dog walking:	Disturbance of game or livestock can be a problem, no conflict with other activities, no facilities required.
Children playing:	Vandalism can be a problem, no conflict with other activities, no facilities required.
Horse riding:	Trampling is serious on heavy soils, designated routes are needed to avoid conflict with others, fencing and waymarking routes is preferable.
Jogging:	Environmental impact low, no conflict with other activities, no facilities required.
Wildlife observation:	No environmental impact, no conflict with other activities, no facilities required.

4.3 What facilities do common activities require?

The seven common activities can take place in woodland without any special facilities, although some are considerably enhanced by the provision of amenities, such as table and bench units for picnicking, and improved surfaces on rides and footpaths for walking. In contrast, children playing positively relish unimproved sites; muddy surfaces and puddles to sink the wellies in or splash though on bikes. Appendix 1, parts 1—5 gives sources of detailed designs and advice for woodland owners considering provision for the common seven activities, at basic levels. Specialized facilities for children playing are considered below and for wildlife observation in Chapter 5. Appendices 3, 4 and 5 contain sources of labour, funding and conservation advice which apply generally to all the schemes in Chapters 4 and 5, and consequently are not referred to through the text. Landowners are strongly recommended to seek professional advice in relation to the development ideas outlined below and in Chapter 5. This is particularly important in relation to the commercial viability of the more capital-intensive projects (see Appendix 1.1.14) and for good quality landscape design, especially for any buildings (see Appendix 1.1.15).

4.4 What potential do the minor activities have?

As mentioned at the end of Chapter 3, the activities less common at the moment may grow in popularity if they are well suited to woodland, if facilities are provided and if they capture the public's imagination. Each activity is now considered in terms of its potential growth, its suitability in woodland at the urban fringe and its facilities required. Sources of detailed advice are given in Appendices 1 and 2 and the appropriate sections are referred to through the text.

4.5 Informal activities: children's play

There is great potential for children's play in woodland near housing areas, or at more rural sites that are popular for picnicking and family visits, or at woodland with overnight facilities. The woodland setting is ideal and can provide the materials for construction, such as round wood, tree branches and sawn timber. Landowners are recommended to use the detailed guidance in a
. recent publication entitled *Providing for Children's Play in the*

Countryside (see Appendix 1.5.2). Among other things this outlines the value of natural environments for play, as follows:

Natural environments are beneficial to children and provide new opportunities for play.
Play in the countryside helps to open up an understanding of the fundamentals of life.

Play areas should use the natural resources of the site, such as trees, water, landform, etc., and need not include man-made attractions, although if provided these are often very well used.

One example of how a woodland can be used as the setting for some imaginative play ideas has been developed by David Hayes at his Landmark Centre at Carrbridge in the Highlands of Scotland, and is described in more detail in Chapter 6. Whilst tourists are the main visitors to this site, the ideas are equally applicable to woodland in the urban fringe. Apart from the usual complicated apparatus which the Landmark staff have built (Plate 6), two very simple ideas have a lot of appeal, a maze and a balancing trail.

Plate 6 — Sophisticated adventure play apparatus at Landmark, Carrbridge.

The maze (Plate 7) is entirely two-dimensional, based on board walks over the heather and, despite the absence of screening hedges, it is no easier to follow. It is of course easy to cheat, but most visitors stay on the boards, no doubt encouraged by the mock tombstones of those who fell by the wayside! The balancing trail is made of logs running at about 500 mm above the ground. Variety is introduced by using both round wood and sawn timber, in both horizontal and vertical positions, and at varying heights (Plate 8). Both these amenities are simple in construction and show what can be done using round wood and sawn timber. It must be emphasized that this type of 'adventurous play area' is only one of several types of provision, and landowners could consider others such as kickabout games areas, and the needs of disabled children as discussed in *Providing for Children's Play in the Countryside*. Sources of design and advice about adventure playgrounds are given in Appendix 1.5.

4.6 Barbecue sites

The potential for these lies at the more rural sites in the urban fringe where there is existing use or demand for picnicking. The activity is definitely catching on at home in the garden, and as the taste for barbecued food grows, it could develop into a picnic

Plate 7 — The boardwalk maze at Landmark, simple to make and great fun.

activity to be charged for as a specialist facility, as in many countries such as Australia. Woodland barbecue sites are rare but are so popular the wardens have to take bookings (Plate 9).

Despite a forester's understandable reluctance to introduce fire in his woodland when so much effort is spent trying to prevent it, the growing trend for barbecues is well-suited to woodland. Provided steps are taken to reduce any danger of fire to manageable proportions, barbecues can easily be accommodated as woodland recreation. Broadleaved and mixed woodland is better suited to barbecues than coniferous woods, which have the highest fire hazard, but given proper provision barbecues can be accommodated even in conifer woodland. Provision has to be made in suitable open areas away from any vulnerable young plantations on specially designed hearths where there is no chance of fire spreading. Restrictions on fire being lit only in approved barbecue places need to be displayed and enforced. It may be necessary to limit the fuel to charcoal or wood provided by the staff, as at Bayhurst Wood, Hillingdon, to stop people collecting their own firewood. At times of extreme fire-risk it may be necessary to close the site altogether. Sources of designs are given in Appendix 1.6.

Plate 8 — The Landmark balancing trail — simpler still, but exciting.

Plate 9 — A barbecue in Queen Elizabeth Forest — the sign explains where to book and limits fuel to charcoal.

4.7 Cycling: BMX

These small-framed, single-gear bikes are growing in popularity and local authorities are beginning to provide competition courses, as at Gateshead. The woodland owner can easily accommodate small informal practice circuits in woods close to urban areas, but the activity can be noisy and may not be appropriate in all locations. The requirements are for gently sloping terrain, some obstacles, natural or designed, on a twisting course, 200 m long, 3 m wide. Sources of detailed advice are given in Appendix 1.7. Such informal courses do not require supervision and are less suited to charging an entry fee than competition courses.

4.8 Cycling: off-road

There is growing interest in off-road cycling which may well be boosted by the arrival of a new design of bike. The 'mountain' bike has a sturdy frame, wide tyres and 15 to 18 gears, and unlike the BMX machine is a full-sized bicycle. Woodland rides, and under-used bridlepaths with reasonable surfaces and easy gradients are most suitable for off-road cycling where they are part of a larger network. Demand for this type of cycling is not going to be confined to the urban fringe, but woodland near towns may well act as the starting or finishing sections of a longer circuit into the countryside. Woodland near town may also be subject to demand for shorter trips and circuits for local children, and this activity does not lend itself to being charged. By permitting entry to off-road bikes, the woodland owner may need to consider special gates or stiles to preclude entry by motorbikes or horses (sources of designs are given in Appendix 1.8).

4.9 Nut, fruit and fungi gathering

It is unlikely that this will increase in popularity other than by responding to new opportunities for gathering when woodland is opened to the public. The gathering is so highly seasonal that it is difficult to see how participation would increase, other than by increasing the resource available, such as adjusting the light levels to encourage brambles. These activities are therefore not very significant and likely to remain highly local in their distribution. It is unlikely that the pick-your-own style of charges could be applied to what Richard Mabey termed 'Food for Free', but an entry fee might be levied at sites where access can be controlled. Landowners' attention is drawn to the possible environmental impact of this activity if carried to excess (see Chapter 9).

4.10 Trail-bike riding

At present this is fairly widespread but involving very low numbers of riders especially in less frequented parts of the urban fringe where riders are unlikely to be observed — and apprehended! Many riders are under the age to ride a motorcycle on the roads, and most bikes are unregistered. The governing body of the sport, the Auto-Cycle Union (ACU), is very aware of the poor public image that results from such unauthorized use, and is anxious to assist woodland owners experiencing the problem. The noise the machines generate, which appears to be an essential part of the fun of 'trail-biking', alienates most other woodland visitors, so specially designated areas are needed if provision is considered at all.

In view of the expense involved in buying a trail-bike, this activity is likely to remain a minority sport. Although numbers may remain low, there is always a demand for practise areas which can be met by 'trail parks' in small woodlands at unfrequented locations out of earshot of local housing. Woodland owners also can consider provision at a more formal level of leasing to a trail-bike club which would provide public-liability insurance. Alternatively, a woodland can be used for specific events and competitions under the aegis of the ACU. In all three cases, trail parks, club use and event use, the owner has an opportunity for earning revenue. The ACU is pleased to advise landowners interested in setting up a trail park, and details are given in Appendix 1.9.

4.11 Trim trail

This has great potential particularly near housing, but more rural sites favoured by joggers may also merit trim trails in view of the distance from town joggers will travel to use a site (10 km). These were first developed in the Netherlands and Scandinavia and are well suited to woodland. They are a series of exercise stations on a trail and provide a more interesting way of keeping fit than jogging (see Plate 5 in Chapter 3). Although trim trails are rare in this country, where they have been installed they prove popular and can easily be constructed from roundwood, as at Linford Wood, Milton Keynes. The Sports Council has produced a guide to the design and use of trim trails, and details are given in Appendix 1.10. It is difficult to see how this activity could bear charging at sites near housing, except where access is restricted to a single entrance and exit.

4.12 Wayfaring

This non-competitive variant of orienteering depends on wooded country and involves navigating between a series of marker posts using a specially prepared map. At present there are around 30 sites in Britain with wayfaring courses, and the sport is likely to grow in popularity with the current interest in fitness. Courses can only be used by visitors who have purchased the wayfaring pack, a map and leaflet of instructions, which provides the land-owner with the opportunity for a little revenue c. 50—80p per pack. Visitors choose from a variety of routes between the marker posts, so that use of the site is not concentrated on one set course. Unlike most activities, wayfaring can involve leaving the paths and the sport's governing body, the British Orienteering Federation (BOF) is very conscious of the potential conflict with shooting and nature conservation. The BOF gives guidance on how wayfaring courses can be arranged to avoid sensitive areas or times. Local orienteering clubs are always willing to help with mapping of the site and designing the course, and the BOF welcomes approaches from any landowner interested in establishing a wayfaring course in his or her woodland (see Appendix 1.11).

4.13 Competitive sports: orienteering

This sport is ideal for large woodlands or mixed country with open space and woodland covering around 500 ha. It is a competitive sport in which some of the challenge is provided by navigating through unfamiliar terrain, and potential use is therefore limited to infrequent events. These competitions can provide an owner with some income: for access or parking, for wear and tear at the assembly point, for concessions for mobile shops, refreshments, or for training. Competitors run individually and choose their own routes, so the course is never swamped with people. As a result, disturbance is at a low but continuous level during the event and trampling is dispersed. The British Orienteering Federation welcomes approaches from landowners interested in letting their woodland be used for an orienteering event (see Appendix 1.11).

4.14 Overnight activities: camping

Woodland is an ideal setting for camping, offering privacy to the campers and screening of the tents to reduce their visual intrusion in areas of high landscape value. The demand for camping lies in two markets, the youth groups like Scouts or Girl's Brigade, and tourism. The demand from youth groups for permanent sites is widespread and can be met by sites in the urban fringe which minimize travelling expenses, and can also be used for one-night or even day visits. The youth group sector of the market does not operate on a commercial basis, and in general, would only be able to provide a peppercorn rent if the site was for local use and with no amenities such as toilets, showers and shop. More sophisticated sites meeting a regional demand for camping may offer the possibility of a higher rental income. Landowners interested in providing a site for youth groups should approach the organizations directly (see Appendix 1.12).

Demand in the tourist sector is more localized, being limited to transit sites near main tourist routes, such as roads to the channel ports, and on the fringe of tourist destinations, like York, Oxford and London. There are also opportunities for sites in more rural areas to act as tourist attractions in their own right, for example Brokerswood, see Chapter 6. The woodland owner has the choice of operating such a site himself and providing the amenities, or leasing it to a club, such as the Camping and Caravanning Club, which would operate the site and provide rental income. The Club is keen to find new sites and welcomes approaches from private owners interested in developing a campsite, whereas the National Federation of Site Operators (NFSO) would be pleased to advise landowners interested in running a campsite themselves (see Appendix 1.12).

4.15 Caravanning

As with camping, this is particularly well suited to woodland for the same reasons of visitor privacy and minimized visual intrusion. The demand lies in the same areas as tourist camping, namely near major tourist routes and destinations, and also as a destination in its own right in the more rural parts of the urban fringe. There are three types of site: club sites, private enterprise sites, and 'certificated locations' which are private sites restricted to five touring caravans. The certificated locations may be of particular interest to the private woodland owner, as they provide an income in return for minimal facilities, a supply of fresh water, and a chemical toilet disposal point, for example at Brokerswood, see Chapter 6. Access is restricted to club members only and 'certification' is done with either of the caravan organizations, the Caravan Club or the Camping and Caravanning Club, which welcome approaches from woodland owners interested in certificated locations (see Appendix 1.13).

For the larger sites there are three approaches that the two clubs adopt: the purchase and development of the site; to advise the owner on development and to lease the site; or to advise on development and to manage it for the owner. Unlike the development of a site by a woodland owner himself, the clubs enjoy a right to change the use of land to a caravan site, under the General

Plate 10 — Co-operative Woods Caravan Site, a large well-appointed site, convenient for London tourists.

Development Order, but planning permission is still required for any buildings that are erected.

On the outskirts of London the Caravan Club operates a popular tourist site in woodland which is rented from the local co-operative society. The site occupies 3.6 ha which caters for about 300 caravans and provides toilets, showers, laundry area and electrical hook-ups (Plate 10). The site's popularity is due to its location near both the Dover road, which is the primary caravan route for the Continent, and a suburban railway station which facilitates sightseeing trips to London. The location of these larger sites in relation to demand and existing provision is critical and the clubs are anxious to ensure that a new site fills a gap in the market. Where such a gap exists, the larger site does offer the woodland owner the opportunity of considerable income, and the clubs are interested in discussing potential sites with woodland owners. Alternatively, landowners interested in running a caravan site themselves should approach the National Federation of Site Operators (see Appendix 1.13).

4.16 Chalets, cabins

These are also well suited to woodland for the same reasons as camp and caravan sites. The potential for this type of development is principally in the more rural parts of the urban fringe and where tourism is important. They offer a holiday in a quiet natural environment and also act as a base from which the tourist can explore the regional attractions. The potential of a site depends both on its location and on the range of regional tourist attractions being sufficient to justify the tourist staying for a week or more. If the woodland is enhanced with its own on-site attractions (see 5.7, Holiday woodland) it can counter the deficiencies in a region. Landowners interested in this type of development should approach their regional tourist board and the NFSO in the first instance to discuss the potential market for the site (see Appendix 1.1.14). Design details are given in Appendix 1.14.

4.17 Field sports: field archery

This is a minor sport with rather limited appeal at present, but demand is growing. It is one of the few recreation activities which require a wooded site and clubs are willing to rent a course provided that they have exclusive use of the woodland for events and

Plate 11 — Grafton Park Wood, a pheasant shoot but open for parking and picnicking.

no public right of way exists, for example Brokerswood, see Chapter 6. If a course is sufficiently challenging for national events, a considerably higher rent is chargeable than if it is merely for local club use. The sport's organizing body, the Grand National Archery Society, is pleased to put woodland owners in touch with local clubs to assess the suitability of the site and the level of demand (see Appendix 1.15).

4.18 Shooting

Shooting needs no introduction to landowners, but the special situation of the urban fringe bears examination. Whilst the overall number of shotgun licenses is remaining fairly constant, the demand for shooting is greatest near major centres of population. Good shoots close to town command high rents and even farms very close to town can make money from pigeon shooting on a day-ticket basis. Of the various types of sport, pheasant shooting and rough shooting (for wood pigeon, pheasant, partridge, woodcock and rabbit) are most suited to an urban fringe woodland. Deer stalking (principally for roe, but sometimes fallow or muntjac), is not suitable as the stalker needs to be totally alone in view of the risks involved in using high-velocity rifles in woodland.

Pheasant shooting and rough shooting are compatible with public access given a little organization to segregate the two in distance or time. Game-rearing and releasing areas need to be kept separated from public areas, and access may need to be managed by confining the public to footpaths or restricting dogs to the lead. There is an interesting example of informal activities being accommodated in a shoot on the Duke of Buccleugh's Boughton Estate outside Kettering, described further in Chapter 6. Grafton Park Wood (80 ha) is open for picnicking and informal activities most of the year but closed to the public at certain times for game management in April and September (Plate 11). Access is not confined to the footpaths although the age of the wood (about 30 years old) means that penetration of the plantations is not inviting.

Pheasant shooting. The potential for pheasant shooting as a managed sport is limited to the more rural parts of the urban fringe where disturbance is lower and where large areas (300—400 ha) of woodland and farmland can be managed for game. Such

areas in one ownership facilitate the management of an organized
shoot, but elsewhere if co-operation between neighbours is difficult, management is limited to less intensive methods such as
woodland improvement or just encouraging wild birds with grain.
A lot depends on the attitudes and habits of local people. Some
shoots very close to towns are little troubled by poaching and
disturbance, a position enjoyed by the Boughton Estate which
has five good shoots, despite adjoining Kettering.

Rough shooting. The potential for rough shooting in the urban
fringe is greater than for pheasant shooting, since the quarry
species are generally more tolerant of disturbance. Pigeon shooting
is very popular in the urban fringe, especially round the big
conurbations, as in Kent and Essex, Warwickshire and Cheshire.
Woodland owners have the opportunity for income from rough
shooting, and those wishing to assess and improve their woodland
for any form of shooting should approach the game advisory
services (see Appendix 1.16).

5. HOW CAN URBAN-FRINGE WOODLAND BE USED MORE IMAGINATIVELY?

The previous chapter outlined the present trends and potential
'growth activities' for urban-fringe woodland, but what other
more imaginative or enterprising uses could be accommodated?
Bearing in mind the current roles of urban-fringe woodland as a
local exercise area or as a specialist amenity, are there additional
roles a woodland can play? For example, environmental education
is largely ignored by the private woodland owners, and yet there
is great potential for local schools to use the natural resources
nearby rather than travelling to rural areas, especially during the
present squeeze on government spending.

How can foresters and landowners capture the imagination of
both school children and the wider public to communicate something of their enthusiasm and feeling for trees and woodlands?
Are there certain groups of people who are not catered for with
the existing styles of facilities and site layout, for example the
elderly or infirm and disabled? Can woodlands be made more fun
for both children and adults? Can visitors be given a broader

experience of woodland? What follows are suggestions for future uses of urban-fringe woodland, most of which could occupy small woodlands of under 10 ha or areas within larger woods, where several themes could be combined.

5.1 The adventure woodland

This combines various play activities on one site, with zones to segregate the various activities listed in Table 5.1 below. As its role is a specialized play area, it is more suited to woodland near housing, or at more rural sites with a large population of weekend visitors. In either setting, if access can be restricted the owner has the opportunity to charge for entry, although this may only be worthwhile at weekends. The site can also be hired in part or whole to youth groups, on weekdays or in light summer evenings.

Table 5.1 — Activities and facilities for an adventure woodland

Toddlers' playground: (Appendix 1.5)	Sand pits, water areas, simple play apparatus, seats for parents nearby.
Adventure play area: (Appendix 1.5)	Play apparatus, ranging from balancing trail, maze, to junior 'assault course', etc.
BMX practice circuit: (Appendix 1.7)	For event practice and or more informal fun on a bike in rough terrain.
Cycle trail: (Appendix 1.8)	On-site circuit for local play, or linked to larger network outside.
Riding: (Appendix 1.3)	On-site circuit for young riders, with horses for hire at stables on site or brought in at weekends and school holidays.
Trail-bike circuit: (Appendix 1.9)	Not suitable near housing, circuit to include obstacles etc., coaching on site, machines for hire.
Woodcrafts: (Appendix 3.1)	Coaching in woodman's skills, courses, day events to generate an understanding of woodland management, to appreciate the site more, to have fun and help.

An adventure woodland close to housing and acting as the local playground need not have toilets, snack kiosks or a car park, although such amenities would improve the attractiveness of the site. More rural woodland mainly dependent on weekend trade will require these ancillary facilities, and include provision for some coach parking. Sources of detailed designs are given in sections of Appendices 1 and 3 as indicated in Table 5.1.

5.2 The fitness woodland

This is a specialist facility to meet the demand from the current interest in keep-fit and combines a variety of fitness facilities with coaching and with a kiosk/snack bar specializing in health snacks, like muesli bars, and yoghurt. By assembling an attractive range of facilities on one site with restricted access, the landowner has the opportunity to charge for entry. As with the adventure woodland, this would find a ready market near housing, but judging from the popularity of woodland jogging such a specialist site may well draw people by car from 5–10 km, so more rural locations also may have high potential. Early morning exercise is feasible for those living near enough to change before work, but can be popularized with showers and a 'health-food' breakfast on site. Special events and coaching can promote new or uncommon activities such as Chinese shadow-boxing and oriental martial arts. The suitable facilities are listed below in Table 5.2 and would in most cases require zoning in separate areas of woodland, to avoid conflict between activities.

Table 5.2 — Activities and facilities for a fitness woodland

Trim trail: (Appendix 1.10)	Exercise stations (press-ups, parallel bars, etc.) on a self-contained circuit.
Jogging network: (Appendix 1.2)	A series of courses, soft surface, well drained, with opportunities for route variation.
Wayfaring course: (Appendix 1.11)	A network of marker posts scattered through the site, requires *c.* 100 ha minimum, not all wooded.
Cycling circuit: (Appendix 1.8)	Suitable on larger sites (60 ha +), unless well connected to outside network. Hire of mountain bikes for more strenuous terrain, a possibility.
Riding: (Appendix 1.3)	On-site circuit and surrounding bridleways, horses for hire at stables on site, or brought in at weekends.

Like the adventure woodland, sites very close to housing do not require toilets or car parks, whereas such amenities are essential at sites in more rural settings. Ancillary facilities include a health food kiosk, showers, and lighting to extend the period of use of the trim trail or jogging circuit at dusk and dawn. On very large sites with 300 ha of woodland and open country, there is also the opportunity to include a permanent orienteering course for competitive events, which can bring in occasional income. Sources of design details are given in sections of Appendix 1, as indicated in Table 5.2.

5.3 The equestrian woodland

This brings the equestrian centre into the woodland, or provides the bridlepaths for a nearby centre. It aims to solve one of the main problems facing the urban-fringe landowner, horse trespass. By leasing the riding to an equestrian centre, over whom the landowner has control under the lease conditions, horse trespass can become a policing duty of the lessee. It is clearly in the lessee's interest to ensure that riders do not stray from the leased bridlepaths and that unauthorized riders do not use the woodland. Where horse trespass is less of a problem or individual riders are few, an alternative approach is to issue permits to the riding centres for a fee, but allow any individual rider to use the bridlepaths free of charge. This is preferable to issuing permits to individual riders which necessitates some level of policing by rangers to prevent unauthorized use. Techniques of dealing with horse trespass are discussed in Chapter 11.

The woodland site also can screen the large buildings for indoor training, provide a network of bridlepaths on site for practising, and long open rides or firebreaks can be used for gallops. With the intensive use that equestrian centres generate, ride maintenance is a serious consideration and woodland on heavy loams or clay soils are unsuitable in view of the expense of surfacing a network of bridlepaths (see Trampling 9.6). In small woods (under 10 ha) which can only accommodate the centre, its open-air training ring and short bridlepath circuit, the idea is only viable if there is a well-developed external network of public bridlepaths, or the potential for a network of permitted routes over the owner's estate.

The location of such a centre is determined more by a gap in the market than by distance from housing or access. Where the provision of equestrian centres is already high, woodland owners can consider leasing riding to an existing centre and still gain the benefits of income and ordered riding. Where a bridleway (i.e., right of access) already exists through a woodland the riding public can be excluded from the leased bridlepaths if the two do not join up, or if they connect, by locked gates to which the tenant has the key. Sources of detailed advice are given in Appendix 1.3.

5.4 Providing for the elderly

Despite the use of urban-fringe woodlands as popular exercise areas, little provision is made for the elderly visitor, who unlike others has more time for regular visits in woodland near housing. A generous provision of benches near entrances, and short 1—2 km walks within the woodland suit the elderly visitor. Part of the enjoyment of a visit to a wood is sitting and watching others more active, or talking with other regular visitors. Benches for the elderly visitor need to be higher than average as it is not so easy for them to get up and down from low seats (sources of designs are given in Appendix 1.17). Particular attention can be paid to walks over easy terrain used by the elderly visitor, to ensure that tree roots are not a hazard to the poorly-sighted and any steps have clear edging with handrails on long flights. At charged sites the elderly visitor could be given free or concessionary entry especially during weekends when charging is worthwhile for other visitors.

5.5 Providing for the disabled

As with the elderly visitor, woodland in the urban fringe, especially where close to housing, can be a valuable resource for the disabled visitor, because it is conveniently located. At first sight there being so many roots to trip over or branches to collide into, a woodland visit does not seem promising for those with a visual or mobility handicap. By providing special facilities or modified designs the disabled person can be given access to woodland and examples of provision are given below in Table 5.3. The Countryside Commission has produced an invaluable detailed guide to providing for the elderly and disabled in the countryside. Landowners are strongly recommended to obtain a copy, which is free of charge (see Appendix 1.17).

Table 5.3 — Modifications to accommodate the disabled

Car parks	:	Specially wide bays close to the pedestrian entrance.
Toilets	:	Wheelchair access, handrails, extra width.
Paths	:	Smooth surfaces, special kerbs, extra width, ramps instead of /or in addition to steps, handrails.
Stiles/gates	:	Special bays to allow wheelchairs.
Seats	:	Higher than average, with backrest.

5.6 The woodland restaurant

At woodlands with vehicular access and a particular attraction, such as a view or setting of high landscape quality, owners should consider the potential for a restaurant which makes a feature of its woodland location. Barbecued food under a pergola or in the open can be a speciality, or a whole-food/health-food restaurant to compliment a fitness woodland. Another woodland theme that can be a selling point is the 'woodman's cookhouse' with old-fashioned recipes such as rabbit stew — though squirrel pie may not be acceptable as many visitors regard such animals as pets. Except where other attractions can provide a 'captive' on-site market, for example the camping and caravan sites at Brokerswood (see Chapter 6), the restaurant's viability would depend on selling its woodland setting to best advantage. Less sophisticated catering in the form of tea-rooms or kiosks with sheltered sitting-out areas are especially suitable where a site is used regularly through the week by joggers, walkers and elderly people. Sources of information are given in Appendix 1.18.

5.7 The holiday woodland

Urban-fringe woodlands near popular tourist destinations such as London or Oxford have potential for holiday accommodation. Ideally this needs to be not too far from one of the trunk roads or motorways and preferably near public transport for easy access to the city centre. The buildings can use both the screening effect of the trees and the woodland atmosphere so that the woodland setting is used sensitively and to advantage. Good examples of how this can be done are the forest cabin/chalet parks developed by the Forestry Commission in rural areas popular with tourists (Plates 12 and 13). Other urban-fringe sites may lend themselves to forest

Plate 12 — Forestry Commission holiday chalets . . .

Plate 13 — . . . a design in sympathy with their woodland setting.

lodges, hostels or motels with building styles using the woodland setting, but without being too contrived.

The holiday woodland can also be developed as a resort in itself with further capital investment such as a leisure centre with considerable facilities ranging from trim trails to a sub-tropical (28°C) 'swimming paradise', as developed by the Dutch. They promote holidays at these 'Centre Parks' in this country so there is an opportunity for a woodland owner with an attractive well-located site to break into this market, either on his own or by leasing the site to a developer. Obviously some careful market-research is necessary for any investment in this league for the opportunity and the style of development to be assessed. For example, in more rural locations of high landscape quality, time-sharing might be appropriate. Whilst a sub-tropical swimming paradise might prove attractive, it is hardly using the woodland setting except as a screen, and landowners can think in terms of the less capital-intensive alternatives, utilizing the woodland resource for adventure play, fitness, riding and interpretation as outlined in this chapter. Early discussions with the local tourist board are strongly recommended (see Appendix 1.1.14), and sources of detailed information about chalet design and time-sharing are given in Appendix 1.14.

5.8 The educational woodland

Environmental studies at school used to place emphasis on field trips to distant locations in the countryside. The focus has now turned to the child's own environment to generate understanding and appreciation of familiar local resources. Woodland owners can think of education as a marketable forest product, as local education authorities (LEAs) will look favourably on developing sites for educational use in the local vicinity of a school, or group of schools. Education authorities have on their staff environmental education advisers who will be pleased to hear from any landowner willing to allow educational use of his or her woods. The owner's degree of involvement can vary from no personal educational role, to composing educational material and leading classes, according to his or her enthusiasm and skills, but most people can communicate a little of their favourite subject, and a range of approaches is indicated below in Table 5.4 and in several of the woodland examples in Chapter 6.

Table 5.4 — Degree of owner involvement with education

Advising LEA of woodland's availability.
Advising LEA staff and teachers of site's resources, potential.
Giving introductory talks to children.
Giving guided walks to children.
Preparing teachers' packs of information, projects.
Preparing leaflets, booklets, workbooks for children.
Providing classrooms, laboratories or even accommodation.

Depending on the degree of involvement, the landowner has the opportunity of charging for entry and for materials, workbooks, and so on. Important ancillary facilities are toilets, a place to park the coach the children arrive in, and a shelter large enough to hold a class of 40 for introductory talks or longer use when it is wet. Where involvement is with nearby schools, the landowner has the opportunity to explain about forestry and the value of woodland to the very audience who may otherwise be trail-bikers, or BMX riders or potential 'lumber-jacks' common to urban-fringe woods. By understanding the value of woodland in the urban fringe, the youngsters may take a more positive view of it, as a resource to be cherished. Educational themes, sources of advice and materials are given in Appendix 2.

5.9 The interpretive woodland

'Interpretation' is a technique for explaining a subject to the layman to enrich the experience of his visit. In the longer term it has the same aim as education: to foster a positive, appreciative attitude towards the resource. Through interpretation landowners can transmit something of their enthusiasm and feelings for woodland and thereby nurture, over a period, a sympathetic attitude in their visitors. It is, therefore, a key subject of this book.

Over the last ten years the common approach to interpretation has been the nature trail and less frequently the visitor centre, which can range from a simple information kiosk, to large buildings with static displays, audio-visual shows, classrooms, sales outlets, cafeteria and toilets. Although visitor centres are more expensive than nature trails, they provide that vital ingredient: a point of contact between management and the public. To be successful, interpretation in the urban fringe must take account of two very important and common attributes of the audience: regular visitors and a wide range of social groups.

On returning to a location, visitors seldom repeat a nature trail or visit to a centre (except to show friends and relatives). Urban-fringe woodlands have a high proportion of regular visitors and therefore nature trails and visitor-centre displays need to be changed, if they are to maintain interest beyond their novelty period. This can be done with a cycle of trail guides or displays which can be changed through the year to reflect the seasons or explain current management operations.

In the urban fringe, because of their proximity to both housing and good urban public transport, woodlands are accessible to a broad range of social groups (in comparison to more rural locations). This provides landowners with the opportunity of reaching a wider audience. However, nature trails and wordy displays in visitor centres appeal most to a minority of the population at ease with the written word as a method of communication. If the wider audience in urban-fringe woodlands is to be reached, other methods of communication need to be used. Landowners must capture their visitors' imagination and make full use of the great advantages of being out in the woodland where:

There is first-hand experience, immediate and memorable;
Vision is three-dimensional;
Senses of smell, taste and touch can be used;
The subject matter surrounds the visitor, and reinforces
    the sense of the presence of nature.

In the urban fringe the regular visitor is the target audience, and various approaches can be adopted to reach this group, for example:

A programme of guided walks;
One-day events covering special topics;
Seasonal advice on what's changing in the wood this week;
An identification service, reference collection and books;
Seasonal displays of woodcrafts and forest methods.

The best method of interpretation is personal contact because it has the great advantage of allowing the visitors to respond to the interpreter and interact with the subject. In return the interpreter is able to adjust the style of presentation to the needs of the visitors, their level of interest and existing knowledge, unlike other methods involving written or audio-visual presentation which are aimed at the theoretical average visitor. Whilst this incurs the expense of staff or the owner's time, it can start at the modest level of occasional guided walks, as at Hockeridge Wood, Hertfordshire (see 6.1). At a slightly higher level of involvement, owners can stage irregular one-day events with displays or demonstrations, such as household wood products or woodland crafts.

Ideally, personal contact is established at a visitor centre, which at the basic level, need only be manned during peak visitor periods. The importance of the centre is that it acts as a focal point for regular informal contact between visitors and management. At its simplest, it need not be elaborate or purpose-built, but can be accommodated in an unused corner of an existing building or in a prefabricated shed. The important point is its location which must be in or near the woodland where visitors can easily find it, not in a distant part of the estate where a building happens to be vacant.

The visitor centre can be used to provide seasonal advice on what is changing in the wood this month or this week, using notices, displays and above all direct contact by the staff or owner. Visitors are often interested to identify things they have seen on their visit, and a centre can provide an identification service with both reference books or specimens, and through personal contact. The experienced forester can make a point about identification, such as the notched needles of silver firs, with much more impact, than if the visitor ploughed through a key.

The visitor centre can also be used as a sales point for woodland produce, as at Brokerswood, Wiltshire (see 6.5). In the urban fringe where visitors are regular, there is the opportunity for placing orders for products like house name-plates, garden furniture and other rustic items, to be collected on a future visit. In addition to woodland produce, the centre can also sell environmental and identification books, posters, etc., to capitalize on the interest generated by the displays and identification service. Operating a tea-room or refreshment counter within a centre can also bring in income both directly, and indirectly if it is located beyond the sales point.

Visitors do not want to be subjected to a bewildering display of new facts which they try to absorb for a few moments, then 'switch off'. If interpretation on nature trails or centre displays is linked to a story line in local history or a sequence of events, it is more easily absorbed and understood. The woodland owner should aim to spark off interest and enquiry, which will gradually lead to increased understanding. Visitors can be encouraged to use all their senses — the feel of the bark, the smell of crushed pine needles; and to awake their emotions — the excitement of walking round a corner and surprising a deer, or waiting expectantly in a hide or observation platform. Man is a ground-living animal so only views trees from below and cannot experience the canopy. David Hayes has recognized this and installed a tree-top trail at Landmark, to take the visitor into the canopy of the Caledonian pine forest on an elevated walkway (Plate 14). The sense of time associated with mature trees fascinates many visitors — "These trees were planted at the time of Waterloo". Equally attractive is linking the use of the site to local history, legends and the oral tradition, such as the owner's family or his staff — "my family have been woodsmen here for five generations". Examples of interpretive themes, methods and sources of designs for hides etc. are given in Appendix 2.

Introducing sculpture to the woodland setting is another way of stimulating the visitor to appreciate his surroundings, pioneered by the Forestry Commission at Grizedale Forest in the Lake District. A more recent example has been set up by David Hayes at Landmark in conjunction with the Scottish Sculpture Trust (Plate 15). The Forestry Commission took the concept a stage further and commissioned a young sculptor, Jamie McCullough, to create a woodland experience, Beginner's Way, a path in Exeter forest, which is not publicized, but designed to be stumbled across. Natural-wood sculptures surprise the visitor, varying light levels in spruce and broadleaved woodland are used to theatrical effect and a delicate catwalk suspension bridge, "an all but invisible spider-web hung from a single thread", challenge the visitor. Woodland is an excellent setting for a sculpture park and is certainly an attraction as the Commission and David Hayes have shown. Other possibilities are in drawing, painting and photography, at both the creative level and the appreciative level. Ideas like this can provide visitors with a new perspective of woodland to stimulate their interest and capture their imagination.

To summarize, landowners should note that in the urban fringe interpretation cannot be limited to the more passive approach of

Plate 14 — A tree-top trail gives the rare experience of being in the canopy.

nature trails and visitor-centre displays, but has to involve more interaction with visitors. It rarely presents opportunities for generating much income above its operating costs, and sources of advice are given in Appendix 2. What interpretation does provide is a less quantifiable but very valuable long-term benefit for the owner, a sympathetic public. As demands for recreation increase and new activities become popular over the years to come, the landowner with a sympathetic and supportive public will have the least problems. The ultimate level of public involvement and commitment is the community woodland, where the public plays an active role in management, and this is the next topic.

Plate 15 — Sculpture in the woodland stirs the imagination.

5.10 The community woodland

To involve the public in woodland management is a bold experiment that is being tried by a few landowners. It draws both on the public's enthusiasm for physical work in the open air and their growing interest in learning country skills. The project fosters a sense of pride in the woodland, and a stronger feeling of participation which can be employed to defend a woodland against misuse by others. In the urban fringe where woodlands are used for recreation by a large number of regular visitors, a landowner has the opportunity to strengthen the link with this community through management. Landowners already find regular visitors to their woodlands often act as extra pairs of eyes and ears and report something suspicious or of interest, without prompting. The community woodland builds on this role of unofficial warden and assembles a nucleus of people interested in learning new skills, managing the woodland and safeguarding its use.

The Woodland Trust has tried such an experiment in community management at Pepper Wood outside Bromsgrove and, contrary to expectations, a very wide range of people joined the management team. An officer of the Trust has prepared a management plan and carries out more specialized silvicultural operations, but the volunteers implement the plan (see 8.3 Recreation management). The volunteers have been properly trained in the skills of woodland crafts by attending courses run by experts from the British Trust for Conservation Volunteers (BTCV). When working in the wood, the volunteers are covered against personal injuries by a block insurance policy held by BTCV. This concept has great potential in the urban fringe because of the regular clientele, and it offers the landowner a method of reducing costs of management both in forest operations and maintenance or improvements for recreation, education and interpretation. Sources of advice are given in Appendix 3.

Having explored what woodlands can offer in terms of outdoor recreation, Part I concludes by outlining the operations of several pioneering landowners involved with woodland recreation.

6. EXAMPLES OF WOODLANDS DEVELOPED FOR RECREATION

At present very few private landowners are involved with woodland recreation but those who are have tackled it often with great imagination and enthusiasm. What follows is a brief outline of several of these operations indicating the different approaches and interesting ideas the landowners have developed.

6.1 The low-key approach — Hockeridge Wood, Hertfordshire

This 63 ha mixed uneven-aged woodland is in the Chilterns 1 km outside Berkhamsted, which experienced *de facto* access from the 1930s onward. It meets local demand for walking, dog-walking, jogging and limited riding, but there is no car access and camping and fire-lighting are not allowed. The wood contains both rights of way and permissive paths, and access is only restricted to the young plantations with a post and single wire fence.

The wood experiences few problems; occasional roadside dumping, a little theft and vandalism, like destruction of rodent traps, and while poaching is not a problem because of the lack of game, two local people are licensed to shoot squirrels and the edible dormouse. Many regular visitors to the wood act as unofficial wardens and report any incidents or unusual events.

Two or three times a year the managing agent conducts guided walks to explain what forestry work is being done. The need for some short-term change in the scene until the coniferous nurse trees are removed is emphasized to visitors. Groups on such walks include local schools and societies. In addition the forester is well known to regular visitors and many stop to ask about forest crafts and operations.

No charge is made for entry and no amenity grants have been sought, since no specific work has been done for recreation other than as a by-product of silviculture. Hockeridge Wood illustrates how low-key recreation and education are easily accommodated within a woodland where the primary aim is still a commercial crop, while retaining an attractive woodland landscape. It costs the owner little in financial terms but some broadening of the woodland objectives which combine with the enthusiasm of the forestry consultant, managing agent and forester results in the successful integration of forestry, amenity, education and public access.

6.2 The capital-intensive strategy – adventure and interpretation woodland – Landmark, Carrbridge

This 30 ha piece of native Scots Pine woodland off the A9 trunk road, 10 km north of Aviemore is in no way urban fringe, being in the heart of the Highlands. It does show however what can be done with a relatively small woodland given plenty of imagination, and in the case of the adjoining visitor centre, plenty of capital (£200 000 in 1970!). The woodland at Landmark has been developed as an additional attraction to the visitor centre, which experienced a drop in patronage when the improvements to the A9 meant Carrbridge was by-passed. The development of the woodland has resulted in visitors staying longer, from about an hour previously to 1½ hours with the new facilities, the adventure play apparatus and tree-top trail. The A9 improvements are a good example of how an external factor can alter the market for a recreation site, as discussed in Chapter 7.

Whilst Landmark's tourist visitors are not typical for most urban-fringe woodland, other sites in the more rural parts of the urban fringe receiving a high number of picnickers can still employ the pay-to-enter approach adopted at Landmark. Sites closer to urban areas can also charge for entry to an adventure woodland where the standard of facilities is high and there is no nearby competition.

In the case of Landmark, where nearly all the visitors are tourists, local people are allowed in free to exercise their dogs, and regulars know the boundary fence merely runs beside the car park and is incomplete! Landmark does demonstrate the imaginative development of woodland and therefore has been used for several illustrations in this book (Plates 6, 7, 8 in Chapter 4; Plates 14 and 15 in Chapter 5).

The adventure woodland area also contains a sculpture trail and a nature trail, the latter explaining the ecology of the native pine forest. The wood is scheduled by the Nature Conservancy Council as a Site of Special Scientific Interest, but the recreation development is compatible with conservation because trampling has been minimized by the full network of boardwalks which discourage visitors from straying into the wood. The wood is not managed for a timber crop, or used to provide wood for play apparatus.

Landmark is unique in combining art, recreation and nature conservation in a way which is both compatible with its pine-wood setting and as a successful commercial enterprise. It does show an exciting way forward in the field of woodland recreation that is applicable to the urban fringe.

6.3 Visitor management and ranger services — Rothiemurchus Estate, Aviemore

Just south of Landmark, near Aviemore, is the Rothiemurchus Estate of the Grant family. This large estate covers some 80 km² of the Cairngorm area which is very popular for outdoor pursuits, particularly climbing, hiking and winter sports. The land ranges from the tundra vegetation of the Cairngorm plateau to extensive forest areas including naturally regenerating Caledonian pine woodland of nature-conservation importance. Other enterprises include red-deer farming, high quality beef production, a trout farm and recreation.

To minimize the impact of visitors on the estate, the Grant family assisted with Scottish Countryside Commission grants have developed an old school-house as a visitor centre to explain about the various enterprises. This exhibition is in the form of a light-hearted but thought-provoking cartoon, the panels of which outline each enterprise. The visitor centre also includes a shop, toilets, an auditorium and is the base for the ranger service.

The key section of the visitor-centre display concerns the 'preferred routes' to limit access to certain areas during deer culling (September—October) and calving (May—June). A free tri-lingual leaflet is available giving the same details in a handy form for the hiker and climber, and reflects the multi-national nature of the tourist market here. The leaflet also contains a modified country code in three languages dealing with the special circumstances of a highland estate in a popular tourist area. For example, campers and caravanners are asked to stay only in approved locations, and motorists are asked to park only in the car parks provided.

The ranger service is grant-aided by the Countryside Commission for Scotland (see Appendix 4.2) and is aimed at increasing the visitors' understanding of the estate, their enjoyment of its amenities and dealing with visitor problems or misbehaviour. The service provides farm tours by tractor and trailer, early-morning bird walks, forest walks, film and slide shows which include the Caledonian pine forest, among other subjects. Over the eight

years during which the service has operated incidents involving
visitor misbehaviour have declined by 75 per cent.

Whilst Rothiemurchus is not an urban-fringe estate, despite the
rapid development of Aviemore as a major tourist centre, it does
illustrate how a positive approach to visitor management, drawing
on Countryside Commission aid, can successfully integrate recreation with a multi-enterprise estate. The light-hearted but effective
display of the estate enterprises, the channelling of visitors along
preferred routes, and the provision of interpretation and visitor
management with ranger services all contribute to the success of
this integration.

6.4 Integrating recreation and education on a large estate –
Boughton Estate, Kettering

Unlike Rothiemurchus, Boughton Estate can be truly described
as urban-fringe, occupying about 45 km² on the outskirts of
Kettering. The house and grounds are run as a tourist attraction
and entry fees are charged, although the East Midlands has no
major tourist magnets and most of the patronage is local. Parts
of the estate closest to Kettering are freely open for walking,
dog-walking and jogging, whereas Grafton Park Wood further
into the countryside has been developed for low-key picnicking
with a few tables and benches which the estate staff constructed
(at a quarter the retail price).

The wood is also one of those very rare places where those in
wheelchairs can be taken for a long woodland walk along smooth
paths. No charge is made for entering the picnic wood, but access
is restricted in April and September for game management, as the
wood is one of five syndicated shoots on the estate. A roadside notice states whether the wood is open or closed (Plate 11,
Chapter 4).

The woodland is not intensively used and may have 500 visitors
on a busy Sunday, and this level of use is entirely compatible with
its principal uses for forestry and as a keepered shoot. Access is
not confined to the paths as the age of the mixed plantations of
pine and hardwoods discourages stand penetration. The access
road has been improved and is the only item which received
grant-aid from the Countryside Commission.

Whilst the Boughton Estate receives its share of urban-fringe
problems, e.g., dumping, trail-bikes and burnt-out cars, the owner,

the Duke of Buccleuch, has developed the educational use of the estate as a long-term answer to these problems. The Duke also has a strong belief that notices and signs should always be positive rather than negative, wherever possible. There are two styles of educational use: estate open days preceded with teachers' briefings for which the estate charges the pupils entry, and *ad hoc* school visits arranged with estate staff or tenants, for which no charge is made. The estate used consultants to prepare a guide book and school workbooks at junior and middle levels, and at open days draws heavily on general assistance from an extremely helpful County Council Countryside Officer and his staff, and also from the Northamptonshire Naturalists' Trust whose members arrange conservation displays.

The estate also uses MSC community enterprise labour for conservation tasks at Boughton, like repair of field walls and planting roadside trees. Horse riding is not a great problem as there are few informal riders who are mostly known to the estate staff. A permanent cross-country course is provided for ponies, in conjunction with the local Pony Club. Some woodland is zoned for nature conservation and access to these areas is discouraged by the keepers who include a significant element of public relations in their work, and are equipped with radios. Permit access to the conservation areas is granted to local naturalists at no charge, and as at Hockeridge Wood, the Boughton staff find that regular visitors to all parts of the estate act as unofficial wardens.

The Duke of Buccleuch and his staff at Boughton have shown how the problems of the urban fringe and pressures for recreation can be dealt with in a positive way using a combination of estate resources, County Council assistance, commercial enterprise and government grant-aid or manpower. The educational approach developed at Boughton is undoubtedly the best long-term invest-ment in public goodwill and understanding that an estate owner can make.

6.5 The integrated woodland approach – the Woodland Park and Countryside Museum, Brokerswood, Westbury, Wiltshire

In the countryside 5 km outside Westbury, the Phillips family has been quietly pioneering an approach to woodland management over the last 20 years which fully integrates timber production, nature conservation, recreation and education. Whilst close to

Westbury, the setting is more rural than urban-fringe, and Tony Phillips does not have to contend with problems of motor bikes, dumping or vandalism to any significant level.

The principal enterprise is timber which aims to bring back into production a heavily cut-over 50-ha oak/ash woodland with some hazel coppice, supplemented by conifer planting to produce an interim return. As much of the stock is young timber, produce is in the form of roundwood, rustic furniture, name-plates, bird boxes, fencing and firewood, all of which are on display and visitors are encouraged to buy. The woodland is in two parcels on either side of a road, with the owner's house and public access area being in one parcel and the other being let for restricted access, camping for youth groups and field archery. The woodlands are managed for nature conservation, with rides kept wide to allow a rich flora to develop which in turn is good for butterflies. Bramble is used to encourage the public to stay on the paths, leaving the stands as reservoirs for wildlife.

The recreation and educational enterprise is multi-use, and the only entry route, past the woodland office, facilitates charging the general public for access. Table 6.1 below shows the wide variety of enterprises and educational projects that the Phillips family has developed with such enthusiasm. The siting of two CEGB pylons in the restricted access wood, despite preventing the development of high forest along the wayleave, has been turned to good use as a permanent campsite for the local Scouts and for coppice and Christmas trees. The compensation for the pylons allowed Mr Phillips to excavate the 2-ha lake in 1959, which also acts as a forest reservoir.

Mr Phillips is particularly keen to promote understanding about forestry, nature conservation and woodland crafts. A collection of craft tools is on display in the wood-yard and the existing, though now disused, saw-pit is realistically displayed with two dummy sawyers (Plate 16). The Countryside Museum is a registered charity and is housed in a pair of converted prefabs joined together, which saved Mr Phillips the expense of a new building, although they are heavy on maintenance. The Museum displays were undergoing renovation during 1984 in the hands of a skilled team from the MSC community enterprise scheme (Plate 17). Visitors to the campsite, caravan site and the general public are all encouraged to visit the museum which is strategically sited

Plate 16 — The realistic saw-pit display at Brokerswood.

between the main entry and the lake. The family designs and produces a range of leaflets for general or specialist visitors telling them of the attractions of the wood, and how to make the most of their visit.

It is clear that the Phillips family members have a great commitment to their integrated approach, which provides income from the various recreation and forestry enterprises. Such an integrated approach is equally applicable in the urban fringe, with the particular mix of enterprises dependent on the qualities of the site as discussed in Chapter 7. The demonstration of fully integrated forestry at Brokerswood is a model for others to emulate in a modified way according to their own interests and woodland attractions. Brokerswood has had no government grant-aid and has received MSC manpower support only this year. Its success is due to the imaginative approach and high personal commitment of Tony Phillips and his family.

Plate 17 — The Countryside Museum at Brokerswood.

Table 6.1 — The Woodland Park and Countryside Museum, Brokerswood.
Facilities for recreation and interpretation

Informal activities
Walking — marked trails, leaflet.
Picnicking — woodland glades provided with tables and benches.
Barbecueing — lakeside barbecue grills.
Camping — Camping Club site with water, bathroom and toilets.
Caravanning — 'Certificated Location', water, bathroom and toilets.
Tea-room — lunches, teas, suppers.
Shop — environmental and tourist publications, charts, sweets, etc.

Specialist activities
Fishing — 2-ha lake, carp, day permits.
Scout campsite — near pylon line wayleave, leased to local group.
Field archery — course leased to local club.
Assault course — course used by local groups.
Holiday cottage — overlooking the lake.
Bed and breakfast — in the Phillips' home.

Interpretation
Countryside Museum — displays, reference books, collections.
Guided walks — Mr Phillips conducts walks for societies, schools.
Supper evenings — groups taken on evening walks and given supper.
Dawn chorus visits — conducted by a local ornithologist.
Lectures — for teachers, societies and the public.
Labelled trails — informal nature trails, extensively labelled with
       features of interest.
Tool exhibition — in the wood-yard.

Part II of this book shows in practical terms how to open your woodland, assess its potential, select a management strategy, and what techniques to adopt.

7. ASSESSING THE RECREATION POTENTIAL OF YOUR WOODLAND

The development of a woodland or series of woods for recreation begins with an assessment of the potential of the site, firstly in terms of external factors such as counter 'attractions, local population, and secondly in terms of the site's intrinsic merits and disadvantages, for example, in extensive glades, but on a clay soil.

7.1 External factors

A number of factors within the regional setting of a woodland can have a marked effect on its potential for recreation in general, or certain activities in particular. The area of influence around an urban-fringe woodland or estate can be divided into three concentric zones with increasing distance from the site:

$$0 - 5 \ \text{km} \qquad \text{local zone;}$$
$$\text{over} \ \ 5 - 30 \ \text{km} \qquad \text{district zone;}$$
$$\text{over} \ 30 - 50 \ \text{km} \qquad \text{regional zone.}$$

The first two zones need to be examined carefully for the external factors such as local population, whereas the third zone need only receive a more cursory investigation, particularly in relation to alternative attractions. The various external factors that affect site potential are outlined below.

Alternative attractions. To avoid saturating the market all similar facilities, particularly wooded parks, country parks, national parks, Forestry Commission recreation sites, and all camping/caravan sites need to be located and plotted on an overlay map. Facilities in the district and local zones may have a particularly important influence on the demand for woodland recreation. For example, the location of stables and riding centres in these two zones is important, but not in the regional zone as riders do not normally travel great distances. Conversely, other facilities such as camp-sites have wider catchments and can influence each other from greater distances, so camp-sites and caravan sites need to be identified in all three zones.

Table 7.1 lists the facilities that could affect the proposed development and which need to be identified in each zone. For facilities with a limited demand like camp-sites, it is important to

locate the competition in a wide area, whereas for a trim trail
demand is more widespread and only more local competition
is significant.

Table 7.1 — The importance of locating alternative attractions

Facility	Local zone	District zone	Regional zone
Riding centre/stables	**	*	
Picnic sites	**	**	*
Adventure playground	**	*	
Barbecue sites	**	**	*
BMX circuits	**	*	*
Off-road cycling	**	*	*
Trail-bike area	**	*	*
Trim trail	**	*	*
Wayfaring course	**	**	**
Camp site	**	**	**
Caravan site	**	**	**
Field archery course	**	**	**
Pheasant shoot	**	*	*
Rough shoot	**	*	*
Orienteering area	**	**	**
Chalet park	**	**	**
Theme park	**	**	**
Country park	**	**	**
Town park	**	*	
Arboretum	**	*	*
Gardens	**	*	*
FC woodlands	**	*	*
Nature trails	**	*	*
Visitor centres	**	*	*

** Very important   * Important

Sensitive uses. Some adjoining or nearby land uses may be sensitive
to the noise and disturbance of certain forms of recreation. In the
urban fringe the noisiest activities are large gatherings of picnickers
and the traffic they generate, children playing, trail-bike riding and
shooting. Where adjoining land uses include hospitals, residential
areas and nature conservation areas, the more noisy forms of
woodland recreation are inappropriate.

Access and transport. All external connections to the woodland need to be identified and the information collected varies in each zone of influence. In the local zone all connections, ranging from paths and bridleways to motorway intersections need to be identified. Canals and rivers are also important where these are navigable and can bring visitors to the site. In the local zone, all forms of public transport (bus, train, metro, or underground connections) need to be checked and their frequencies and week-end services recorded. In the district zone, main road networks and public transport routes together with their origins and destin-ations (the A–B highway) need to be recorded. In the regional zone, the trunk road and motorway network needs to be recorded, particularly in relation to tourism, for example the ports or main attractions such as York or Stratford. Planned developments to the road network in all three zones need to be identified as these can bring new visitors or equally take away existing trippers if the area becomes by-passed (see Landmark in Chapter 6).

Negative influences. Certain land uses have effects sometimes far beyond their boundaries like airport noise, industrial air pollution, the smell of a sewage works. Such uses obviously affect the potential of a site and need to be identified at the planning stage before the mix of activities is selected. Table 7.2 below lists the land uses and their effects, which are always important in the local zone and sometimes in the district zone.

Table 7.2 – Negative influences of nearby land uses

Land use	Effects
Airports	Noise, important for horse riding.
Rubbish dumps	Smells, pests, noise of machines.
Nearby industry	Noise, air and water pollution.
Motorways) Express railways)	Noise.
Sewage works	Smell.
Pylon lines	Visual intrusion, bird hazard.

Population. The local population has a strong influence on the potential for development (with the exception of the potential for tourist developments such as camp-sites, caravan sites and chalet parks). In the urban fringe where catchment areas are small, the local and district zone populations, their size, age groups, car ownership and social group will influence the popularity of a recreation scheme. The type of population obviously is of most importance for schemes involving a lot of capital, like the Woodland Restaurant, but of lesser significance for low-key developments such as a wayfaring course, or for ideas that are always popular, like path improvements and a few benches.

Woodlands which have a population of over 1000 people living within a 2 km walk will be popular for the common activities associated with public open space — walking, dog-walking, jogging, riding and playing. Where there is a large proportion of younger couples starting families, facilities for children's play and keeping fit will be popular. If a large number of elderly retired people live locally, special provision of well-made paths with plenty of benches can be considered. Woodlands with few people living within a 2-km radius, such as those in green-belt areas, are going to draw only the mobile car-owners unless public transport is good. These woodlands may be less suited to a public open-space role and more to specialist uses or attractions which have wider catchments. A trim trail can appeal to the car-owning executives fighting off middle-aged spread. Barbecue sites and picnic sites linked with play facilities can draw picnickers from the district zone or the regional zone.

Social class is also important particularly for the population in the local zone which may even live next to the woodland. Riding, because of its expense, is more popular in more affluent districts, whereas other activities like dog walking are popular with all groups. Woodlands near large populations of inner-city families removed to estates on the outskirts of town seem to face the biggest problems of vandalism and theft. It is in these situations that the owner faces the greatest challenge to generate some sympathetic use of his woodland through education and interpretation.

Demand for recreation is the aggregation of the individual demands of large numbers of people. Many factors affect demand and it is hazardous to try to predict or quantify it. The key point emerges that the role of public open space will be fulfilled nearest urban areas, and more specialist or half-day trip activities will be drawn to sites further afield. Landowners should not be afraid of conducting a little market research themselves; a sample interview with 30 households near the site, or with 30 current visitors could indicate whether a facility might be popular. Using such indicators in conjunction with the analysis of alternative attractions, transport infrastructure, and negative influences, a picture can be built up of the possible gaps in the 'market'. The Tourist Boards and local planning departments may be able to assist with this assessment by providing data or appraisals (see Appendix 1.1.14).

7.2 On-site factors

A number of on-site factors which influence the potential of a woodland for recreation need to be identified and these can be grouped together under the following headings: physical factors, access factors, constraints and opportunities, hazards, special features, services, existing recreational use and problems. In each group, the items need to be identified and plotted on a series of maps or overlays from which a picture of the site's potential will emerge.

Physical factors

Terrain. Contours obviously affect the recreation potential of the site, but most activities have a very wide tolerance of slopes and only very steep slopes (over 50°) are limiting, like along rivers and scarp slopes. Even these areas have some recreation potential and can be zoned for low intensity uses such as wayfaring or wildlife observation. The detailed requirements of individual activities are given in the Reading University Report [8], but in general most activities require gently rolling terrain to provide interest or exercise.

Soil. Clay and heavy clay loams are significant constraints on woodland recreation, and particularly for riding or to a lesser extent walking if the area is very well used. Table 7.3 lists the activities and development ideas constrained by heavy soils, without expensive surfacing and site formation work. Light sandy soils may be liable to erosion on steep slopes if they are heavily used, so they too can constrain the recreational opportunities. Wet areas and spring lines also can limit the potential of an area in a very localized way by causing deviations to paths or the expense of drainage works.

Table 7.3 — Activities and development restricted by heavy soil

---

Activities not recommended
Riding   At any intensity
Adventurous play areas
BMX circuit   )   Unless planned as sacrificial route to
Trail-bike circuit   )   protect the rest of the wood
Trim trail
Camp site
Caravan site
Adventure woodland
Fitness woodland
Equestrian woodland
Holiday woodland   Unless well provided with indoor facilities

Activities acceptable at low intensity use*
Walking   About 30/day/km of ride
Dog-walking   About 30/day/km of ride
Picnics/barbecues   About 10/day/ha of picnic area
Jogging   About 15/day/km of ride
Playing   About 15/day/ha of play area
Wildlife observation   About 30/day/km of ride
Off-road cycling   About 10/day/km of ride
Gathering fruit, etc.   About 30/day/km of ride
Wayfaring   About 5/day/ha of whole wood
Field archery   About 30/day/km of ride
Orienteering   About 1000/event
*The figures are for the activities *on their own*; managers should designate
a route for each activity.

Activities entirely compatible with heavy soils
Woodland restaurant (a surfaced car park is needed)
Community woodland management

Area and shape. The size of a site obviously limits its potential,
with under 10-ha woodlands being restricted to single activities,
whereas larger ones (10—50 ha) can support a range of activities,
perhaps zoned in different areas. Even very small woodlands of
under 1 ha have potential for some uses, like a 'certificated location'
for five touring caravans. All activities have minimum area requirements and by grouping these into classes, an indication of the
potential of various sizes of woodland can be derived. Obviously
activities feasible in the smallest woodland can be accommodated
either in zones of larger woods or expanded to fill the site available;

for example, a 1-ha woodland can accommodate several small picnic sites of 200m² and no other uses, but a 10-ha woodland can accommodate several large sites of 2000m², in combination with dog-walking on the rather limited path network, and other path users, walkers and riders, passing through.

To give a crude indication of the potential of the various sizes of woodland, Table 7.4 lists the activities which are restricted to

Table 7.4 — Activities and development restricted by woodland size

Woodland under 1 ha

On-site activities
Gathering fruit, etc., small picnic/barbecue site, wildlife observation, children's play area, informal BMX circuit, informal trail-bike circuit, walk for the elderly or disabled, small tent site, small caravan site (5 vans, certificated location), community woodland management, field study site for one school.

Linear activities passing through
Dog walking, walking, jogging, riding, off-road cycling.

Woodland 1−10 ha

On-site activities
Any of those listed above; large picnic/barbecue sites, trim trail, large tent or caravan site with full amenities, shooting, restaurant, educational use for several schools, interpretive woodland.

Linear activities passing through
As listed above.

Woodland 11−50 ha

On-site activities
Any of those listed above; adventure woodland, fitness woodland (without wayfaring), equestrian woodland, holiday woodland, field archery.

Linear activities contained on-site, or passing through
Dog walking, walking, riding, jogging, off-road cycling.

Woodland 150 ha +

On-site activities
Any of those listed above; wayfaring, orienteering only on sites of 300 ha+, fitness woodland.

Linear activities contained on-site, or passing through
Dog walking, walking, jogging, riding, off-road cycling.

minimum sizes of woodland. It is useful to distinguish between
'on-site' activities such as playing or picnicking which are centred
on an area, and 'linear' activities which use a path or track such as
walking and riding, which may pass through smaller woods but be
contained on longer circuits in larger woods. The shape of the
woodland is also important in relation to its potential for recreation. Long thin woods may have more length of track than
compact blocks of woodland, but are less able to accommodate
activities needing large areas, for example the holiday woodland
chalets, or to provide a sustained woodland experience.

Glades and open areas. Although area and shape are significant,
the recreation potential for on-site activities is really governed by
the extent of the glades and open areas in a woodland. These are
what most visitors use, and whilst new glades can be opened up
expressly for recreation or as a by-product of silviculture, the basic
potential lies in the existing glades and open areas. The penetrability of the stands is another factor to be taken into account
as mature trees over a clear forest floor obviously have much
greater potential than pole-stage plantations. In mature woodland
with a clear floor, the 'open areas' for recreation effectively
extend under the canopy throughout the wood, and mature beech
woods for example, have a higher potential than mature oak
woods with more undergrowth. Glades, open areas and areas of
free access under mature timber need to be mapped to assess the
potential of the site. Large open paddocks in a woodland setting
are particularly significant for certain activities, like picnicking,
large-scale camp sites and special events.

Woodland type. The species and age of trees have little effect on
recreation potential in comparison to the influence of glades and
open areas. These areas are where most activities take place and
the stands of trees act mainly as a backcloth (see 2.2). Whilst there
has been a considerable public outcry against conifers being
planted in the uplands, this attitude does not deter people from
using conifer woodland for recreation. On the outskirts of London,
for example, Buckinghamshire County Council manages over
300 ha of mostly coniferous woodland at Black Park which
attracts over a million visitors a year.

Woodland type, however, does affect the attraction of a woodland. Larch and other deciduous trees with light foliage have a less oppressive effect than the dark green of most conifers, and this is particularly important at low light levels. Similarly the silvicultural treatment the woodland receives can incręase light levels through thinning, brashing and pruning, to make a woodland more inviting. Light levels also have an indirect effect on the attraction of a woodland by influencing spring flowers, autumn colours and bird and insect life. For this reason mixed woodland, deciduous woods and active coppice are all more attractive to the visitor than pure stands of conifers (or young hardwood plantations). Such attractions can be significant, by extending attendance beyond the summer months, or by providing teaching material for educational visits. Woodland type, age and silvicultural treatment also affect the penetrability of a woodland, and this can vary within a wood with stands of different ages and species. The most significant woodland types in this context are mature beechwoods and conifer woods with clear forest floors, which allow access throughout the stands, not just in open spaces.

Internal access. Access to the site has been discussed in Section 7.1. Internal access includes entry points (for cars, horses and pedestrians), rights of way for pedestrians or riders, and circuits on the existing network of paths and rides. The number of access points is very significant when it comes to considering the possibilities of charging for entry, or 'defending' the woodland against unwelcome visitors, like trail-bike riders. Circulation patterns are important in relation to the potential of the site to contain visitors walking, riding or cycling, because the smaller sites rarely have the potential for circuits as indicated in Table 7.4 above. The location of the access routes on the site is also significant as woodlands with peripheral access routes can experience greater problems of refuse dumping, or visitors trespassing on neighbouring land. (The management techniques to deal with these problems are discussed in Chapters 8 and 10.) Any potential or existing car-parking areas need to be identified as on-site car parking is critical for some activities, like picnicking.

Constraints and opportunities. The potential of the woodland for recreation may be constrained by conservation objectives or other existing land uses. Where woodland is ancient coppice or ancient high forest, or has some other importance for nature conservation like nesting birds of prey or rare lichens, its potential for recreation may be limited. A nationwide conservation survey of woodlands is currently being carried out by the Nature Conservancy Council and landowners are urged to contact the NCC for professional advice (see Appendix 5). However, where a site is of conservation importance, the recreation proposals may be directed towards interpretation and education. In larger woodlands, recreation may be compatible with conservation by zoning the woodland into sensitive and usable areas or times. As most visitors remain on the paths or in open areas, disturbance to wildlife can be minimized although there are obvious exceptions, like terriers getting 'lost' down badger or fox holes. Management techniques to minimize environmental impact of recreation are discussed in Chapter 9.

Shooting can constrain the recreational use of a woodland, but contrary to the general view, it is compatible with regulated public access. Bird rearing and feeding areas need to be segregated from access areas, dogs need to be kept on leads throughout and access may need to be denied at more sensitive times. Similarly forest operations can constrain the potential of a woodland particularly if large-scale felling is imminent, or the current crop is Christmas trees. In these situations the recreation development of a site may be deferred or use temporarily diverted elsewhere, until the operations are completed and the trees harvested. Existing way-leaves for overhead lines and underground pipes and cables also can limit the possible choices of development, particularly in relation to the siting of buildings. There is a positive side to these wayleaves in that plantations are usually not allowed to be grown on them, and therefore they can be turned to advantage as open areas or linking routes for recreation. A wayleave at Brokerswood for example is used for a Scout camp site (see Chapter 6).

Finally, there are impending roads or other government-imposed schemes that can bisect or affect a site so as to impair its re-creational use. Where these are uncertain, recreation plans may need to be deferred until a decision is reached. Alternatively, there may be scope to modify the imposed scheme to allow the wood-land to be developed, such as a bridleway bridge over a main road, or the relocation of an access point. In either case, it is essential to check with the local planning authority at this 'survey stage' whether any such government schemes, or proposals for neighbouring land, are under consideration. When their own proposals have been narrowed down to one or two options (as described in 7.3 Recreation Appraisal below), landowners need to consult the local planning authority about the suitability of their proposals.

Hazards. On-site dangers need to be mapped and fitted into the recreation assessment, as they need to be neutralized or enclosed to prevent access by the public. Hazards are diverse and usually obvious; for example, derelict buildings, mine shafts, quarries, strip-mining areas, cliffs, unstable reclaimed land, old settling ponds and buried wartime ammunition. The latter is particularly significant in view of the current popularity of treasure-seeking with metal detectors. Forestry itself can produce hazards, like old trees shedding limbs especially after prolonged dry spells; old pollards are notorious for this. Water features also cause hazards; for example, undercut river banks, waterfalls, canal locks and sluices, deep ponds, lakes and flooded quarries, thin ice in winter. Properly managed, many of these hazards can be turned into attractions or sources of interest; the history of the buildings or mining activities, the cliff-top views, the rock exposures in quarries, and the obvious recreation potential of water features for fishing, swimming or just admiring, and so these can be also recorded as special attractions (see below).

Special features. In addition to the attraction that some potential hazards can provide, for example rock climbing on cliffs, other special features need to be assessed. These include cultural heritage items, such as buildings, connections of the woodland with history, famous people, local products, or literature, music and art. Other attractions are viewpoints, gardens, an arboretum or trees notable for their age, size or variety, water attractions and other natural features.

Services. The availability of mains services on site and at what distance is significant for any development involving building, like the holiday chalets or an indoor riding circuit. These services need to be noted on the plan, as expensive connections or pollution constraints on sewage disposal can affect the viability of the larger projects. The local planning authority is able to advise landowners about any such pollution constraints.

Existing recreational use and problems. Any *de facto* and authorized recreational use needs to be recorded and assessed as to how
it uses the site. *De facto* use may offer useful clues as to the
possible demand for more formalized recreation schemes. It may
also point to potential problems which need to be solved, such as
trespass by horses in the plantations as a result of a boggy bridlepath. Other problems to be recorded here are the usual urban-
fringe ones; poaching, trespass, vandalism, theft, dumping, arson
and deviant behaviour, which will require controlling under the
recreation management plan. (Management techniques for dealing
with these problems are discussed in Chapters 8–11).

7.3 Recreation appraisal

From the information uncovered in mapping the recreation
potential of the site, a series of development options can be
derived and tested against the owner's objectives, which may
then be re-evaluated. For example, a maturing woodland with
high potential for a caravan site may lead to a modification of
the silvicultural treatment in favour of small felling coupes to
provide glades for the caravanners, instead of clear felling in
large coupes.

Criteria. Landowners need a set of criteria by which they can
judge the suitability of the various options that have been evolved
from the site survey. The primary goal is to develop the recreation
potential of the woodland, or group of woodlands, within the
limits imposed by the certain criteria which minimize the impact
of the recreation on the estate, adjoining land, and the environment. Landowners may wish to amend or add to the criteria
outlined below according to their particular circumstances, objectives and level of interest.

1. Any recreation development must be compatible with the
   owner's other objectives for the woodland and surrounding
   land or water (reviewed in the light of the recreation potential
   of the site).
2. Any recreation development must be compatible with any
   existing use of the site or adjacent land or water, not under
   control of the owner.
3. Any recreation development must be compatible with the conservation of nature on the site and surrounding land or water.

4. Any recreation development must comprise a compatible mix of activities.
5. Any recreation development must reflect the owner's level of commitment and the financial resources available to him.
6. Any recreation development must reflect the needs and desires of the surrounding population as far as is possible within the limitations imposed by the other five criteria above.

Landscape design. Landowners need also to select the urban or rural style of development they prefer for the special circumstances of their woodland. The guiding concept is that visitors are often attracted by the quiet natural setting a woodland provides, and by its special qualities of stature, shelter, screening and age, outlined in Chapter 2. In close proximity to urban areas, such qualities take on special significance and the development style should utilize these qualities to the full, rather than urbanize the woodland. Occasionally, the style of development may be more urban as in the case of the woodland restaurant described in Chapter 5, or noisy rather than quiet, as in the case of a trail-bike circuit.

It is important for landowners to adopt a style of development and detailed designs acceptable in terms of visual impact as well as environmental impact. Strong urban styles for buildings or fixtures such as fencing look inappropriate in a woodland setting. Equally important is the need to avoid designs that are too rustic and look contrived, for example home-made picnic furniture using massive tree trunks rarely looks functional and is often very uncomfortable. Landowners are strongly recommended to seek the advice of a landscape architect to help with the selection of development styles and detailed designs compatible with a woodland setting.

After selection, a short-list of recreation options compatible with the owner's objectives can be subjected to a financial appraisal and discussed with the tourist board (see Appendix 1.1.14), with labour-providing bodies, such as the MSC schemes (see Appendix 3), and with grant-aiding bodies (see Appendix 4) to assess the owner's level of contribution. The various levels of owner involvement for the recreation ideas discussed in this book are the subject of the next chapter. With the choice of options further reduced by the financial commitment required, the final choice or choices can be informally discussed with the planning authorities prior to working up detailed designs and costings for formal submission for planning consent. Landowners are strongly recommended to have early discussions about their proposals with the local planning authority. Not only can this avoid re-designing unsuitable schemes, but certain proposals, such as new bridleways, will be closely aligned with the authority's own interests and may result in support, such as manpower from countryside management teams (see Appendix 1.1.16). Detailed design advice is available from a variety of sources listed in Appendix 1 for recreation, Appendix 2 for education and interpretation, and Appendix 5 for nature conservation. A check-list of the procedure to produce a recreation plan is given in Table 7.5 below. The following chapters consider the management strategies and techniques involved in implementing the recreation plan.

Table 7.5 — Recreation plan check-list

---

1. Define current objectives for woodland (7.3).
2. Assess potential of woodland.
2.1 Examine external factors (7.1): alternative attractions, sensitive uses, access and transport, negative influences, population.
2.2 Examine on-site factors (7.2): terrain, soil, area and shape, glades and open areas, woodland type, internal access, constraints, hazards, special features, services, existing recreational use and problems.
2.3 Prepare a series of developmental options from the information revealed in 2.1 and 2.2, the ideas outlined in Chapters 4 and 5, and using specialist advice from the sources listed under each activity in Appendices 1 and 2.
3. Consider whether the objectives defined in (1) need to be revised in the light of the recreational potential revealed in 2.3 and revise as necessary.
4. Test the development options (2.3) against the revised objectives (3) and select those options most compatible.
5. Examine the compatible options (4) in terms of their level of owner involvement of capital and management (Chapter 8) and select those most appropriate.
6. Carry out an outline financial appraisal of the selected options (5) using advice from the local planning department and regional tourist board for marketing aspects (Appendix 1.1.14), sources of manpower (Appendix 3), and sources of finance (Appendix 4).
7. Select a short-list of options from (6) which appear most feasible in financial terms.
8. Discuss the short-list (7) with the local planning authority to assess whether any option requires modification, or would be unlikely to receive planning permission (Appendix 1.1.16).

Table 7.5 (*continued*)

9. In the light of the discussions (8), select the preferred option(s) and refine the designs using specialist advice for activities (Appendices 1 and 2), specialist advice on landscape design (Appendix 1.1.15), specialist advice on nature conservation (Appendix 5) and specialist advice on insurance (Appendix 1.5.4).
10. Refine the financial appraisal (6) of the preferred option(s) using the tourist board (Appendix 1.1.14), sources of manpower (Appendix 3), and sources of finance (Appendix 4).
11. Submit the preferred option(s) to the local authority for planning permission (Appendix 1.1.16).
12. Obtain funds and manpower from sources in (10) and carry out development work to implement the preferred option(s); ensure that any contractors used fully understand the sensitive nature of the woodland environment and the reasons for the preferred style of design (see 7.3 Landscape Design).

8. SELECTING A MANAGEMENT STRATEGY

8.1 The range of options

The various activities and ideas for woodland recreation discussed in Part I of this book range from those that are neither capital nor labour intensive, to schemes like the chalet development which require considerable capital and daily management. In order to give the landowner guidance on the various management strategies that are possible, the activities and schemes for woodland recreation have been divided into five levels of 'owner involvement' in terms of the capital and management required:

> Minimal involvement strategies;
> Low involvement strategies;
> Medium involvement strategies;
> High involvement strategies;
> Very high involvement strategies.

Obviously some activities, like playing, may appear at several levels according to the provision of facilities, site improvements and the management they receive, whereas other developments only appear at high levels, such as the chalet park. The landowner is able to choose the appropriate strategy in accordance with his or her own level of interest, the resources available, and other objectives.

8.2 The five levels of involvement

Minimal involvement strategies. There are two basic approaches. The first is to allow low-intensity informal activities without any facilities or site improvements, and management is only limited to occasional inspections. This approach excludes certain activities because they require maintenance, for example bridleway repairs and fencing for riding, or litter collection at picnic areas. The second approach here is to lease the woodland or allow permit-access to specialist groups like naturalists, archery clubs or even to sell the woodland to recreation developers for schemes like a restaurant or chalet park. In this approach facilities, improvements and management are provided by the club or developer. Table 8.1 below gives an indication of the owner's possible involvement for informal activities, and the division between the owner's and tenant's involvement for leased activities. Owners can, of course, increase their involvement by providing site improvements or amenities with a view to earning a higher rent.

Table 8.1 — Minimal involvement strategies: roles of owner and tenant

Activity/development	Owner	Tenant
Low intensity informal: (under 5 visitors/ha/peak day) Walking, dog walking, jogging, gathering fruit, etc., wildlife observation, playing.	Inspection 4—6 p.a. and litter collection as needed, e.g., 2 p.a.	—
Permit-access: Wildlife observation, educational groups	Permit administration, annual inspection.	—
Leased use/development: Archery course	Lease administration, annual inspection	Club erects and runs course
Youth campsite	Lease administration, annual inspection	Group runs site and erects amenities
Touring campsite or caravan site	Lease administration, annual inspection	Club runs site and erects amenities
Chalet park	Lease administration, annual inspection	Developer erects and runs park
Woodland restaurant, tearoom or kiosk	Lease administration, annual inspection	Caterer erects and runs amenity
Bridlepath network	Lease administration, monthly inspection of rides	Club or centre maintains rides

Table 8.1 (*continued*)

Activity/development	Owner	Tenant
Leased use/development (cont'd.)		
Trail-bike park	Lease administration, annual inspection	Club erects and runs course
Shooting	Lease administration	Syndicate runs shoot
Orienteering	Lease administration, inspection after events	Club erects course, runs events

Low-involvement strategies. At this slightly higher level, a wider range of low-intensity informal activities are possible by providing simple facilities or on-site improvements, such as minor path works, a few seats, or tables and benches for picnics. Management is limited to quarterly inspections except in the case of picnic facilities which need more frequent checks during the summer season to keep them tidy. Table 8.2 below details the owner's involvement for the wider range of low-intensity informal activities, which includes simple provision for picnicking, riding and the elderly, and for specialist activities like BMX-cycling and guided walks. Riding should only be considered for a low-involvement strategy where metalled rides already exist, or where soils are well drained and slopes not steep. There is then no need for costly maintenance.

Table 8.2 — Low-involvement strategies

Activity/development	Owner involvement
Low-intensity informal: (under 5 visitors/ha/peak day)	
Walking, dog walking, jogging, wildlife observation, off-road cycling, playing	Minor path works, drainage, steps, handrails, etc., simple seats, quarterly inspection
Provision for elderly people	Simple seats, quarterly inspection
Picnicking	Few tables and benches, litter bins, car access to grass car park, weekly inspection and litter collection in summer
Riding	Special route, minor ride works, drainage, etc., monthly inspection
Specialist activities: BMX informal circuit	Special circuit on rough terrain, minor path works, quarterly inspection
Education/interpretation	Guided walks

Medium involvement strategies. These cater for more intensive informal activities which require greater or more elaborate provision of facilities and site improvements. At this level of involvement modest provision is made for more specialized activities, like small 'certificated-location' caravan sites which require only water and chemical toilet disposal point. With this more intensive informal use, however, site inspections are required more often, and in the case of picnic areas, litter collection can be a more onerous task, although take-your-litter-home campaigns are becoming successful. At medium involvement, riding can be considered on metalled or natural rides where soils are well drained, or where drainage can be improved. Education and interpretation projects can be broadened to include special events as well as guided walks mentioned above in the low-involvement strategy, but no capital items are necessary. Table 8.3 below details the owner's involvement in providing for more intensive informal activities and modest amenities for specialist uses.

Table 8.3 — Medium involvement strategies

Activity/development	Owner involvement
Medium-intensity informal: (5—50 visitors/ha/peak day)	
Walking, dog walking, jogging, wildlife observation, off-road cycling	Path works, levelling drainage, steps, handrails, etc., simple seats, monthly inspection
Playing	Simple apparatus using natural features, fallen tree, etc., monthly inspection
Provision for elderly or disabled people	Special route with level surface and ample seating, monthly inspection
Picnic and barbecue sites	Tables and benches, litter bins, barbecue grills, grass car park, toilets preferable, weekly inspection and litter collection in summer
Riding	Special route, ride works, especially drainage. Monthly inspection
Specialist activities:	
BMX informal circuit	Special circuit with simple natural obstacles, minor path works. Inspect obstacles monthly
Caravan site	Water supply, chemical toilet disposal point, grass surface. Daily inspection of site and amenities in season
Education/interpretation	Laying on demonstrations, events, guided/self-guided walks, introducing talks

High involvement strategies. This level of strategy provides for medium to high-intensity informal activities with extensive or elaborate facilities, site improvements and more frequent maintenance. At this level, more specialized facilities can be provided, such as fitness woodland, which bring a variety of activities together in one theme. With intensive use, toilets become essential and some limited surfaced parking is preferable. Inspections of apparatus and site cleanliness have to be more frequent, and maintenance of horse rides can involve resurfacing. This high level of involvement allows owners to consider providing for more specialist uses like camping and caravanning on large sites, or increasing their commitment to education and interpretation. Table 8.4 below details the owner's involvement in providing for such intensive informal uses and full provision for more specialist activities.

Table 8.4 — High involvement strategies

Activity/development	Owner involvement
High-intensity informal: (over 50 visitors/ha/peak day) Walking, dog walking, jogging, wildlife observation	Path works, levelling, drainage, steps, handrails, etc., surfacing on wet or heavy soils, monthly inspection
Off-road cycling	Special circuit, path works, drainage, surfacing on wet or heavy soils, monthly inspection
Playing	Adventure playground. Weekly inspection to check apparatus
Provision for elderly or disabled people	Special routes with level surface, seats, ramps, toilet at entry, monthly inspection
Picnic and barbecue sites	Tables, benches, litter bins, barbecue grills, metalled and grass car park, toilets, kiosk, daily inspection of site and toilets in season, site security
Riding	Special routes, ride works, drainage, surfacing, weekly inspection of route and waymarks
Specialist activities: BMX informal circuit	Special circuit with obstacles, natural and purpose-built, minor path works, inspect obstacles monthly
Trail-bike park	Special circuit with obstacles, natural and purpose-built, minor path works, inspect obstacles weekly, course administration
Touring campsite or caravan site	Water supply, toilets, showers, chemical toilet disposal point, site administration, daily inspection of site and amenities in season, site security

Table 8.4 (*continued*)

Activity/development	Owner involvement
Specialist activities (cont'd.)	
Trim trail	Special circuit, exercise apparatus, weekly inspection of apparatus
Adventure woodland	Combined adventure playgrounds, cycling and riding circuits, weekly inspection of play apparatus and monthly inspection of circuits
Fitness woodland	Combined trim trail, jogging, cycling and riding circuits, weekly inspection of apparatus and monthly inspection of circuits
Education woodland	Shelter for class, toilets, coach parking, preparation of talks, guided walks, workbooks, administration
Interpretive woodland	Nature hut, toilets, car parking preferable, preparation of seasonal events, displays, guided/self-guided walks

Very-high-involvement strategies. This level of strategy provides for specialist uses with a significantly higher level of capital works which have been mentioned as leased or sold options in the minimal-involvement strategies. Under these very-high-involvement strategies, the landowner is the developer or joint developer, rather than merely the developer's landlord as is the case with the minimal-involvement strategies. There are four development ideas, the equestrian woodland, the large touring camp and/or caravan site, the woodland restaurant or tearoom, and the holiday woodland of chalets. The degree of involvement for each idea is outlined in Table 8.5 below. Where very large areas (200–300 ha) are being considered, several or all of the ideas in Table 8.5 could be combined as a forestry theme park in which the recreation facilities have a strong forestry connection.

Table 8.5 — Very-high-involvement strategies

Development	Owner involvement
Equestrian woodland	Equestrian centre buildings, practice ring, bridlepath circuit/network, toilets, car parking (all-weather surface), bridlepath maintenance, drainage, surfacing, weekly inspection of circuits and waymarks, centre administration and security

Table 8.5 (*continued*)

Development	Owner involvement
Large touring camp/caravan site	Water supply, toilets, showers, chemical toilet disposal point, shop, electrical hook-ups for caravans, site administration. Daily inspection of site and amenities in season, site security
Woodland restaurant or tearoom	Restaurant building, catering. Daily collection of litter around building, building maintenance
Holiday woodland	Chalets and support buildings, letting administration, building maintenance, site security

8.3 Recreation management

The recreation management to implement these strategies is the subject of this section. The various activities require some degree of management, according to their type and popularity, but basically the tasks can be divided into ranger services and site maintenance. There is a range of management styles which can be grouped according to their increasing input:

Minimal input — lease site for others to manage;

No on-site staff — periodic ranger presence and maintenance, with or without voluntary rangers;

Limited on-site staff — permanent ranger presence supported by voluntary/MSC maintenance;

Skilled on-site staff — permanent ranger presence and maintenance staff.

Minimal input. At the lowest level, sites may be run for private recreation at no cost to the manager, and usually some income. The British Steel Corporation woodland around Corby is let for shooting and access by permit for naturalists, but beyond administering the tenancy or permits the BSC are not involved in recreation management. There is a similar situation at 'Co-operative Woods' (*sic*) in South London which are leased to the Caravan Club by the Royal Arsenal Co-operative Society which takes no part in site management (see 4.15).

No on-site staff. Small urban-fringe woodlands like Linford Wood, Milton Keynes, have no wardens permanently on site, but are inspected by maintenance staff or mobile rangers covering several

sites. The Forestry Commission adopt this approach in their small
urban-fringe woods like Holt Wood, Croydon and Joydons Wood,
Bexley, on the southern outskirts of London. This low-key
approach can be strengthened during the busier summer months.
In Milton Keynes, for example, where the ranger's beat includes
Linford Wood and 1200 ha of linear parks, seven temporary
rangers are taken on to increase the presence on the ground when
it is most needed. Volunteer rangers to advise and assist the public
are used by the London Borough of Bromley in their open spaces
and woodlands, but difficult incidents are handled by the specialist
Park Security Service.

Community woodland, an advanced form of low-key management involving no on-site staff, is being tested by the Woodland
Trust at Pepper Wood outside Bromsgrove. There are no permanent
on-site staff but both ranger services and site maintenance are
carried out by an autonomous group of volunteers drawn from the
surrounding towns and villages. An officer of the Trust has prepared
a management plan and carries out more specialized silviculture
tasks, such as marking thinnings, but the volunteers under their own
committee implement the plan with only limited supervision from
the officer. Early indications of this new approach look very promising, and it could well be applied to urban-fringe woodlands to
increase community involvement and improve the standards of
management in what are sometimes neglected resources (see 5.10,
8.6 and Appendix 3.1).

Limited on-site staff. At the next threshold of staffing the limited
permanent on-site staff are often supported by volunteer or MSC
labour. Volunteers are usually employed on site maintenance
rather than as rangers, for example in Gateshead the local branch
of the Conservation Volunteers carry out path improvements and
bridge building in Thornley Wood and Paddock Hill Wood Country
Parks. The use of Manpower Services Commission schemes to
provide maintenance or ranger staff is another low-key approach.
In Gateshead full on-site wardening of Thornley Wood and Paddock
Hill Wood is provided by two part-time and two full-time posts
funded by the MSC. The 12-month time-limit attached to MSC-
funded posts is a drawback to the scheme as experienced MSC
staff have to move on to allow others to take their places (see
Appendix 3.3).

Skilled on-site staff. The highest levels of recreation staffing have permanent on-site staff dealing with both ranger services and maintenance tasks, but specialization increases with the size of the organization. For medium-sized woodlands (about 40 ha) the role of warden and maintenance staff may be combined in one or two people performing both tasks, for example Bayhurst Wood Country Park, Hillingdon, and the Broxbourne Woods in Hertfordshite. In the larger woods more specialization is needed and ranger tasks are separated from woodland management and site maintenance. The specialization can increase with the size of the organization and certain functions can be provided by roving teams, such as security on large estates with managed shoots. There is also the opportunity to extend the role of existing on-site staff to include ranger work or site maintenance. For example, the forester at Hockeridge Wood and keepers on the Boughton Estate both include an element of public relations in their work (see 6.1 and 6.4). Both Countryside Commissions run training courses for newly-appointed rangers (see Appendix 1.1.12) and can help with costs (see Appendix 4.2).

8.4 Ranger services

The tasks of a ranger fall into three principal groups: site security, public education and management information. The term 'ranger' is now being adopted in the recreation field, to emphasize a wider role than that of 'warden', which implies an overriding concern with site security. The ranger's profession is a young one and is starting to develop an institute to co-ordinate standards and training. Both Countryside Commissions subsidize courses for recently-appointed rangers (see Appendix 1.1.12).

Site security. A ranger, particularly in uniform with an obvious radio, is widely regarded as being of great value in deterring anti-social behaviour and the misuse of woodland. The secluded nature of woodland is one attribute which makes maintaining a reasonable standard of visitor behaviour more difficult than in more open ground. Managers and the Police emphasize that an obvious staff presence, or just their vehicle if suitably emblazoned significantly helps to encourage the proper use of a site. Radios are also highly recommended as they give the ranger in a difficult situation a psychological advantage over the trouble-maker and the very real advantage of being able to summon help. In general, however, when dealing with anti-social behaviour, the educational approach is favoured rather than resorting to applying by-laws, except in the case of persistent offenders.

Woodlands are associated with a wide range of anti-social behaviour but most of this is not linked to the use of the wood for recreation. Such behaviour seems to be more associated with quiet, secluded areas of public open space in urban areas or the urban fringe, particularly areas near large housing estates of relocated people. The anti-social behaviour that can be encountered is divided, in Table 8.6 below, into the rarer incidents involving people and the more frequent problems concerning property.

Table 8.6 — Anti-social behaviour reported in urban-fringe woodland

Rape	Car burglary
Prostitution	Car dumping
Homosexuality	Fly tipping
Flashers	Excretion
Peepers	Vandalism
Suicide	Poaching
Drug taking	Metal detecting
Blackmail	Arson
	Theft of trees, equipment, etc.

Of the rare incidents, flashers, peepers and drug-taking (mainly in the form of glue-sniffing) are the most reported. Most woodland managers do not regard courting couples as a problem except in the forms of prostitution or adultery which can attract black-mailers, as well as peepers. If homosexuals adopt a location as a rendezvous, this can lead to attacks from 'queer-bashing' thugs. Of the more frequent incidents involving property, fly-tipping, dumped vehicles and car burglary, and theft of trees, equipment, fencing and so on are most common. Most problems although serious in nature are occasional, or like theft and vandalism, are sporadic and unpredictable in their outbreaks. Metal-detecting is giving cause for concern, both in relation to disturbance and theft of items of archaeological significance, and in a more dangerous way at sites used for wartime training with live ammunition. The problems of poaching and arson are described in Chapter 9 on environmental impact. To counter these problems, the police and woodland managers advise the following courses of action:

Advertise your presence, with rangers in uniform or with armbands, radios, and with emblazoned vehicles.
Keep a high standard of site maintenance — if a woodland looks cared for it is less likely to attract problems.
Seek the advice of your local constabulary, the crime prevention department.
Train rangers in crime prevention with the help of the local police crime prevention department.
Encourage regular visitors to act as voluntary rangers by reporting incidents or unusual events.
Deny nocturnal access to vehicles to preclude dumping and other anti-social behaviour.
In high risk areas, advise visitors that plain clothes dog patrols frequent the site.
In high risk areas, advise visitors to keep alert, avoid walking alone and report any incidents.
When a serious incident occurs, contact the police to post photofit pictures of suspects, and alert the local press.

Public education. The ranger's duties can include some level of education or interpretive work, depending on the importance the owner gives to these topics. At the basic level of public relations, a ranger has to adopt an educational approach when dealing with visitor impact on both the environment and land uses, and the conflict between activities (see Chapters 9, 10 and 11). The Rothiemurchus and Boughton Estates are examples of this approach (see Chapter 6). Where educational use is the principal role of the woodland, for example at Thornley and Paddock Hill Woods, Gateshead, specialist educational rangers are employed full-time. Where equal emphasis is given to recreation and education, the rangers have a teaching role in addition to their site security duties. Educational involvement can vary from leading occasional guided walks for the public, to running full interpretation programmes for both public and specialist audiences. This educational aspect is regarded by many managers as the long-term solution to site misuse, since it increased public awareness and appreciation of the environment.

Management information. At small woodlands where the ranger service and maintenance roles are combined in a small team of two or three generalists, as at Bayhurst Wood Country Park, Hillingdon, the site manager will have a clear idea of how the public are using the wood from his personal experience as a ranger.

At larger woodlands, or on large estates managing several woods, the specialist role of ranger can provide information for the estate manager. Information such as visitor behaviour, how a site is used and the patterns of use in space and time can be fed back into the woodland recreation plan to adjust it in the light of changing circumstances.

8.5 Site maintenance

Table 8.7 below lists the principal maintenance tasks and their frequency. Most major maintenance is carried out annually in the quieter months or occasionally mid-week during the visitor season, if urgent work is required, such as repairing toilets. Although the magnitude of the tasks varies with the nature of each woodland and the use it receives, repair and improvement of rides and paths is widely reported as the most onerous, particularly in popular riding areas with heavy soils. At most woodlands during the visitor season, maintenance is primarily weekly or daily site and toilet cleansing, depending on the level of use. Sites with picnic areas, being busier and generating more litter than other woodland, have the greater burden of daily maintenance. Woodland managers stress the importance of daily cleansing during the visitor season, particularly at heavily-used sites with major attractions such as large paddocks or lakes. It is argued that sites and toilets stay clean if they start clean, as a little dirt, litter or heavier refuse attracts more of the same.

Table 8.7 — Site maintenance tasks

Frequency	Common tasks
Annually	Repair/reprovision of facilities (tables, benches, signs, buildings)
Annually	Reseed/scarify glades and paddocks
Annually	Repair/improvement to rides and paths
Annually	Repair of gates and fences
Weekly—Daily	Litter collection in popular zones (car parks, picnic areas)
Weekly—Daily	Toilet cleansing
	Unusual tasks
Annually—Monthly	Collection of dumped refuse
Annually	Collection of autumn leaves at camp sites
Weekly—Daily	Provision of fuelwood at barbecue sites
Monthly	Inspection of play equipment

At smaller woodlands without major attractions or facilities where the pattern of use is walking, riding, jogging and children playing, cleansing is not a major task and daily maintenance may be unnecessary. Annual maintenance tasks similarly are less onerous, except for repair to rides which are the main area of visitor impact. Whilst daily litter collection is unnecessary at such sites, an annual or monthly purge of dumped refuse may be required, particularly in woods adjoining roads and housing areas (see 9.7). Woods with unusual use, like the long camping season for London tourists at Co-operative Woods Campsite, have specialized requirements such as the collection of autumn leaves to prevent the grass camping pitches becoming too wet. The daily provision of firewood during the summer for the barbecues at Bayhurst Wood Country Park is another unusual specific requirement.

How the various maintenance tasks are handled depends on the level of management input described at the beginning of this section. At small woodlands with no on-site staff, maintenance may be carried out by a roving team looking after several sites. At sites with a small permanent staff like Bayhurst Wood Country Park, Hillingdon, both daily and annual maintenance may be carried out by the rangers, or restricted to litter collection with specialist staff for other maintenance. At woodlands with larger teams, the staff carry out all routine maintenance tasks, but may use specialist contractors for major works like ride repairs as at Bencroft and Broxbourne Woods, Hertfordshire. Few managers will be as fortunate to have their own supplies of road gravel on site, but many can use their own woodland produce, often as round wood or less frequently as sawn timber where the owner operates a sawmill. When sawn timber is not available from the estate, the production of picnic tables can be put out to commercial suppliers or sawn timber can be bought in for construction on site.

8.6 Finance and insurance

Costs. It is not intended to give detailed costings for the provision of facilities and maintenance, since these are quickly outdated, and vary according to local conditions, such as soils, the availability of sawn timber and labour on the estate. Landowners, however, may be interested in the approximate costs of the more basic

items for the lower-level strategies and Table 8.8 is based on the
experience of Hertfordshire County Council's countryside management scheme.

Table 8.8 — Hertfordshire countryside management scheme:
approximate costings (1984)

Surfacing
Cold planings   £3.90 per ton delivered
Hoggin   £3.90 per ton delivered

Bridleways — hard surface
Planings base, hoggin top, regraded,
surfaced, etc. by contractor   approx. £1000.00 per 100 m

Bridleways — soft surface
Ditch, grade, remove roots, etc. by
contractor   approx. £1500.00 per 300 m
                                                 (but costed by site and tasks)

Note: HCC frequently use their *own* tractors and diggers and buy hoggin,
planings, pipes, etc. only.

Estate and fencing materials
                                                 (Cost not including delivery)
Round posts:
    4" × 6'   Softwood treated   £2.90
    7" × 6'   Softwood treated   £3.80
Square posts:
    4" × 4" × 6'   Softwood treated   £2.60
    3" × 3" × 6'   Softwood treated   £1.50
Oak posts (for signs):
    4" × 4" × 8'   £8.00
Gate posts:
    9" × 9" × 8'6"   Softwood treated   £14.00
    7" × 7" × 8'6"   Softwood treated   £11.00
Gate:
    10' field gate   £40.00
Rails:
    4'2" × 12'6" long   Softwood treated   £3.00
Railway sleepers for bridge deck, etc.   £7.50
Picnic table and bench   *c.* £40.00

Manpower, grants and taxation. In addition to seeking design
advice when establishing facilities, landowners can offset the costs
incurred with manpower, grants and taxation. Appendix 3 gives

details of sources of manpower, and local authority countryside management schemes are commended as being particularly helpful. Appendix 4 contains sources of financial support and advice on taxation as there may be opportunities for claiming tax relief to offset the costs of recreation in woodland.

Revenue. Earning revenue from woodland recreation can be difficult for several reasons. Firstly, it is often impossible to exclude people, and regular visitors are not convinced by partial fencing techniques like the Landmark car park (see 6.2). Secondly, where an urban-fringe wood acts as a park for local residents, it is difficult to charge for an amenity that is freely available elsewhere from local councils, *unless* the landowner has something rather special to offer, such as a trim trail, or an adventure play area. Thirdly, the revenue may not meet the costs of collection, particularly in the case of manned collection points, whereas leased activities can offer a revenue for minimal cost (see Table 8.1 for examples).

Trust-the-visitor schemes. To minimize the cost of collecting revenue, honesty boxes or pay-and-display ticket machines can be used. At Trosley Country Park, near Wrotham in Kent, the County Council find only 1 in 7 visitor groups put the parking fee in the honesty boxes during the week when use is mainly local people, but this rises to 1 in 3 at weekends when more distant visitors use the park. This is particularly interesting as it shows the resistance of the regular visitors to pay for what in their eyes is 'their park'. Landowners with picnic sites may find it worthwhile charging for car parking and simple pay-and-display machines can be hired for *c*. £100 per year (see Appendix 4.5). The National Trust and the Forestry Commission (FC) use these machines (which are similar to platform ticket machines) which can yield a useful income, for example £1000 from the FC Wyre Forest car park. The advantage of using these simple machines, which require maintenance but no electricity, is great in comparison with the expense of manned entrances. Such machines can also be used at pedestrian entrances to woodland, as at the start of a trim trail, if pedestrian access can be restricted to the paying entry point.

Season tickets. In the urban fringe where the pattern of use is one of regular visits by the local population, consideration can be given to issueing season tickets where woodland has a manned entry point or warden patrols. The Woodland Park at Brokerswood, outside Westbury, uses this system as the only entry passes the woodland office (see 6.5). As technology progresses in the next ten years, unmanned turnstiles using plastic 'credit card' passes may become cheaper and allow the landowner to restrict access to permit or season ticket holders without needing to man the gate.

Key clubs. In 1972 the Economic Forestry Group (EFG) launched the Countryside Club which gave access by a key and booklet to 4000 ha of private woodland, provided with simple picnic facilities. Membership was open to the public at £10.50 per year, but it did not grow as hoped, and EFG attribute this to the facilities freely available from the public sector. However, access by key may still be appropriate at the restricted level, for instance a tenant with a wayleave for riding, or other activities with low numbers of participants such as naturalists and teachers. Landowners need to be aware of the potential abuse of this system with keys being copied. Locks with 'restricted issue' keys which cannot be copied in a locksmith's without the landowner's permission, are a solution to this abuse.

Insurance. The two areas of concern are increased fire risk for commercial plantations and occupier's liability for claims by third parties against the landowner. Fire insurance premiums are not normally increased if public access is managed and proper fire precautions are taken (see 9.5). Occupier's liability insurance is strongly recommended as, in 1984, £500 000 cover on a 2000-ha estate cost about £60 per annum. For certain activities leased to organizations or individuals such as a riding centre or a trail-bike club, landowners can insist on the tenant taking out an indemnity to protect the owner from any claim against him.

When volunteers are working in an owner's woodland under a Conservation Volunteers' (BTCV) scheme (see Appendix 3.1), they are covered by a block policy that the BTCV has taken out. Landowners using volunteers not covered by the BTCV scheme should cover themselves against any claim by taking out additional insurance to cover the days on which the volunteers are working. In the case of MSC staff (see Appendix 3.2 and 3.3), the owner's liability depends on whether he or she is the sponsor (i.e. 'employer') of the MSC team, in which case the owner should take out employer's liability insurance. Where the MSC staff are working for someone else, such as a local council, and the landowner is only the client, he or she does not need to take out insurance other than occupier's liability. Chapters 9–11 examine more detailed techniques of recreation management: environmental impact, effects on woodland management and adjoining land use, and inter-activity conflict.

9. RECREATION MANAGEMENT TECHNIQUES I: ENVIRONMENTAL IMPACT

9.1 The recreation management approach

Recreation management has yet to develop into an exact science and as yet management techniques can rarely be quantified. A manager is not operating to detailed specifications such as 25 riders per wet day is acceptable and 26 is not. This level of information is rarely available for patronage except at pay-on-entry sites, nor are the effects and problems caused by different activities known with any precision. Recreation management is carried out more on the basis of responding quickly to problems when they develop and thereby building up a fund of experience on which to base preventive measures, rather than applying site-capacity estimates or other theoretical concepts. However, from the experience of foresters and park managers involved with woodland recreation, it is possible to build up an idea of visitor behaviour, the problems they bring and the counter-measures required. There are three areas of concern: environmental impact; interactions with forestry and adjoining land uses; and conflict between recreation activities. They are the subjects of this and the following two chapters.

9.2 The five forms of environmental impact

To assess the impact of activities it is worth recalling from Chapter 3 what parts of the woodland are used by each activity. Table 9.1 below lists the activities most common in urban-fringe woodland and the parts of the woodland they use (the full list of activities is given in Table 3.1). The table shows the concentration of use on the rides and in glades, with only children's play and wildlife observation using the woodland stands. This distribution of activities within woodland indicates that the principal areas of impact on the resources are the trails and glades, in effect the woodland edge.

Table 9.1 — Woodland areas used by common activities

Activity	Rides	Glades	Stands
Walking	**	*	
Dog walking	**	*	*
Riding	**		
Picnicking	*	**	
Children playing	*	**	**
Jogging	**		
Wildlife observation	**	**	*

* minor use; ** major use

Impact can take five forms:

disturbance to wildlife;
removal or destruction of plant and animal life;
fire;
trampling of vegetation and soil, and
littering.

Of the five, trampling, especially from horse-riding, causes managers most concern and can result in considerable expenditure to repair the damage or reinforce the site to withstand the wear.

9.3 Disturbance to wildlife

Within each woodland, disturbance to wildlife appears to be a highly localized problem because most recreation occurs on rides or in glades, which leaves the woodland stands generally undisturbed. This very limited penetration of the stands, together with the screening and sound-deadening properties of woodland, results in the stands being relative havens for wildlife, separated by corridors of activity. Urban-fringe woodlands are rarely sites of national significance for conservation, and often their value is as an import-ant *local* resource for teaching or as a conservation 'shop window' for the environmental movement. Whilst certain uncommon species, such as goshawk or sparrowhawk, would be sensitive to the public approaching their nests, ornithologists and a recent research paper suggest that most woodland birds, including rarer species like the hawfinch, are tolerant of humans because they can easily hide [5]. Research in Denmark suggests that where roe deer are present and recreation is introduced, bark stripping can increase because the animals are kept from feeding in the rides and glades by human activities [16].

Only two common human activities penetrate the stands, children playing and naturalists, of which the former is more significant both in terms of numbers and noise level. Dog walkers often let their pets run free during a walk, and whilst the owners rarely penetrate the stands, the dogs frequently explore the margins. At sites with deer or during the nesting season in most woods, free-running dogs can disturb the wildlife and dog owners can be asked to control their pets or keep them on leads in certain parts of the woods. Wayfaring and orienteering are uncommon activities which also penetrate the stands, but the British Orient-eering Federation is well aware of the potential problem and advises clubs to design courses to avoid sensitive areas and times.

The ultimate solution to stand penetration and wildlife disturb-ance is physical exclusion, either by fencing or by silvicultural methods. In Thorndon Country Park, Essex, the badger sett in one plantation is surrounded with a 1-m-high chestnut-paling fence, to exclude people and dogs. Such fencing is used on a wider scale in wooded urban parks to discourage access and picking spring flowers, as at Abbey Woods in South East London (Plate 18). The GLC, however, allows free access to the stands in its wooded country parks which are less heavily used, such as Hainault Forest.

At Weald Park, another Essex County Council country park, access to the plantations is discouraged by a 0.3 m 'hedge' of brash (dead side branches are removed prior to thinning) running parallel to the rides, two or three rows into the plantation (Plate 19). Brambles can be used in the same way and encouraged by increas-ing the light reaching the woodland floor through careful thinning. This technique is used at Bayhurst Wood Country Park, Hillingdon, to discourage people straying off the rides in some parts of the woodland. A more impenetrable natural barrier is used at Black Park, Buckinghamshire, where the outer two or three rows of a plantation may be left unbrashed and unthinned, giving the appearance of a thicket, whereas the body of the plantation receives normal silvicultural treatment.

Plate 18 — Fencing to restrict access to spring flowers in a heavily-used urban wood.

Plate 19 — Brash as an impromptu hedge to discourage access to plantations.

Whilst stand penetration is mainly very limited in most types of woodland, there is one exception where stand penetration is the norm. Mature, thinned, woodlands with clear forest floors, for example under beech woods or conifer plantations, permit free access and visitors are not confined to the main rides. The effect of this increased stand penetration on wildlife is not clear and needs to be researched. Stands with a clear forest floor tend to have less animal and birdlife than less penetrable stands with undergrowth, and penetration of mature stands may not disturb the wildlife high in the canopy overhead.

Poaching as an illegal woodland activity does result in stand penetration and disturbance to wildlife in addition to the poacher's immediate quarry, but as reported in the following section, most woodland managers describe poaching as a sporadic minor irritant rather than a serious problem.

9.4 Removal or destruction of plant and animal life

This has two principal forms which might be termed as 'hunting' and 'gathering'. 'Hunting' wildlife, mainly collecting invertebrates and poaching, is widely reported and most of the woodlands examined had suffered from some form of 'hunting' at a low level. 'Gathering' can encompass flower and foliage picking: nut, fruit and fungi collecting; moss, bark and stump collecting for flower arrangements; and firewood collecting. 'Gathering' is also widely reported and like 'hunting' is a minority activity which only occasionally causes problems for management.

Collecting invertebrates, commonly butterflies, is not regarded as a problem unless the site is managed as a nature reserve. However, landowners should consider prohibiting collection of any sort, except with their written authority, to control the impact of this activity on their woodland. The role of the rangers, guided walks and visitor centre displays, can be used to educate the public about conservation of nature. Many managers regard poaching as an 'irritation' due to its sporadic or very low level of activity. Some woods have a local poacher known to the manager, but who has never been caught in the act (which is essential for a successful prosecution). Badger digging and carrying firearms are the only forms of poaching viewed seriously by managers, and in both cases police assistance is considered necessary. Regular visits by rangers and the use of walkie-talkies are the tactics adopted by many managers; in one Tyneside woodland the increased ranger presence led to the local 'terrier club' advising members to avoid the area. Whereas poaching is mainly a management problem, ferreting can be tolerated as a means of reducing the rabbit population.

Of the 'gathering' activities, nut, fruit and fungi collecting can be tolerated in very low numbers, but flower or foliage picking and moss, bark and stump collecting should be discouraged by rangers using an advisory and educative approach rather than any punitive measures. The flower-picking problem principally affects bluebells and primroses and can be tackled with signs ranging from the prohibiting 'Do not pick wild flowers' (in Lesnes Woods, South London) to a more exhortative approach, 'For the benefit of future generations, we ask visitors to leave the flowers where they are' (in Linford Wood, Milton Keynes). Neither approach is claimed to be successful, and most managers see a long-term education programme as the real answer, starting with the current generation of school children.

An occasional commercial variant of foliage-picking occurs where a lorry-load of holly might be taken at Christmas time. (None of the woodland managers interviewed grew Christmas trees near the urban areas as this is inviting theft.) A licensing approach is adopted by Essex County Council in Thorndon Wood, where florists are permitted to take laurel and cypress foliage. Foliage-picking by the public seemed to be sporadic in most woods and one manager believed that it follows evening-class lectures. Ladies collecting foliage are often oblivious to the effects of taking the leading shoots of young trees, having made their selections purely on artistic merit. This is another problem which a ranger can tackle with an educational approach both to the offender and by giving talks to relevant groups like the Women's Institutes.

On a grander scale, tree-felling is most common in woodland near housing and without permanent on-site staff. Such woods function as unofficial adventure play areas for children from nearby housing, and felling trees is part of the adventure. At Thornley Woods, Gateshead, many of the children were known to the ranger and an evening home visit by the local policeman halted the epidemic. The problem appears to be cyclical and will re-appear when the next group of children reach 'lumberjack' age, although Bonfire Night also stimulates felling.

9.5 Fire

Unlike other forms of environmental impact which are limited to the site of the activity, fire can spread rapidly through a woodland and is therefore a most serious problem. The following paragraphs are limited to the recreational aspects of fire protection and land-owners are referred to Chapter 6 in *Forestry Practice* [9] for detailed advice. Discussions with the local fire brigade are particularly recommended where increased access or new activities are being considered.

The fire danger in any wood is governed by a range of factors, such as the age and spacing of the trees, their type (coniferous or broadleaved), the extent of the plantations, the flammability of the ground vegetation, the number of days without rain and the presence of the public. Young conifer plantations are the highest hazard, whereas mature broadleaved and coniferous woods with clean floors have little fuel and are low hazards. In broadleaved woodlands where the fire risk is low, owners can permit barbecues in picnic glades, as at Bayhurst Wood Country Park, Hillingdon. Most managers will wish to ban open fires completely and restrict barbecues to large paddocks and proper grills, as at Thorndon Country Park, Essex. At none of the woods examined was fire reported to be a serious problem, although those with conifer plantations took particular care in their silvicultural methods, especially brashing.

Brash left on the forest floor is one of the main fire risks and a smoker's match or cigarette-end can easily set it alight during dry conditions. Some advocate the more traditional forestry practice of removing the brash completely, leaving a clean forest floor, as at Lickey Hills Country Park, Birmingham. An alternative approach is to collect the brash towards the centre of a plantation leaving a clear floor in the marginal rows of trees. The practice in Essex County Council's conifer plantations is to gather the brash into low 'hedges' every other row into a stand to discourage public access (see 9.3), but these 'hedges' are intercepted at regular intervals to prevent fire spreading along them.

Woodlands with a high proportion of vulnerable young conifers will require a system of firebreaks and water points, a fire plan and trained staff, as detailed in *Forestry Practice*. Where a local authority is the woodland owner, liaison with the fire brigade can result in specialized equipment like Land-Rover fire engines being stationed on site, as at Black Park Country Park, Buckinghamshire. Other woods with lower hazards, however, require appropriately lower levels of fire-fighting capability. The most frequent sources of fire are discarded cigarettes or matches, and children playing or being mischievous. The British Steel Corporation's woods around Corby have most fires during school holidays, despite their woods being open only on a permit basis for shooting and to naturalists. To combat this risk, BSC delay cutting the woodland rides so as to avoid dead grass lying around during the school holidays.

Landowners with commercial crops of timber will insure their conifer plantations against loss by fire, and discussions with insurers revealed that premiums are higher for areas with *unmanaged* public access, but not usually increased if reasonable fire precautions are taken and visitor management is applied. Where a recreation woodland in the urban fringe is one of several woods on an estate, it can be insured as part of a block policy for all the estate woodland, and is not penalized with a higher premium.

Woodland managers with experience of recreation suggest that far from public access increasing the fire hazard, the owner benefits three ways:

> Permitted public use is self-policing as vandals are restrained by the risk of being seen;
> Vandals are likely to ignore 'Private — Keep Out' notices;
> Visitors are likely to report any fires they find, which can go unnoticed in a private wood.

9.6 Trampling

The effects of trampling will be familiar to owners with livestock:

> Loss of ground cover;
> Soil compaction, leading to puddling and root damage;
> Soil erosion, especially on slopes.

Trampling problems are worst on heavy soils, or light sandy soils, and on steep slopes (see also 7.2 and Table 7.3). Trampling is exacerbated in woods as a result of the microclimate under the canopy, or in the shelter beside younger woods. The shade, lower air movement and higher humidity all reduce the rate at which a ride can dry out, thereby increasing the damage by trampling.

Of the common woodland activities, the most significant impact is invariably damage to the surface of woodland rides caused by horses. Table 9.2 below shows the activities ranked in order of the significance of their trampling effects.

Table 9.2 — Significance of trampling by different activities

Horse riding	)	Significant in any number, if weekly
Trail-bike riding	)	or more frequent
BMX riding	)	Significant in modest numbers (under
Off-road cycling	)	100) if weekly or more frequent
Walking/dog walking	)	Significant only in large numbers
Jogging	)	(100s) if weekly or more frequent
Wildlife observation	)	
Shooting	)	
Adventure play	)	Significant only round facilities,
Picnic/barbecue	)	highly localized
Trim trail	)	
Campsite/caravan site	)	
Chalets	)	
Wayfaring/orienteering	)	

Horse riding. Regular horse traffic over heavy soils in wet weather results in poaching of the surface and a widening of the route to avoid the quagmire, as there is the danger of the mud trapping the horse's hoof and causing strained tendons. A variety of methods can deal with this problem: minor works, surfacing and restricting access.

Minor works. In Pepper Wood near Bromsgrove, for example, the clay soil on a sloping bridleway was badly poached by winter riding, and the dense coppice with standards had grown over the ride. The Woodland Trust, which owns the site, plans to increase the width of the ride to let in light and air, whilst improving the drainage to remove surface water. The Trust hope that this will be sufficient to keep the ride passable and reduce horses trampling the forest floor, without resorting to the expense of surfacing the ride.

Surfacing. Where surfacing is necessary, various techniques have been applied. From the rider's viewpoint, what is required is a soft, all-weather, well-drained surface, such as sand, sawdust, bark, or hoggin. In difficult clay soils some degree of site formation may be necessary, as at Linford Wood, Milton Keynes, where the ride was deep-drained on either side, and a sub-base of broken brick laid and dressed with hoggin. The council highways department can provide waste road surfacing (road planings) which forms a good foundation for bridlepaths, as in the case of Broxbourne Woods, Hertfordshire. With much of their woodlands on clay soils, and having a high population of riders in the area, Hertfordshire has severe poaching and trampling problems which would be very expensive to solve without such co-operation.

Restricting access. The difficulty of trying to restrict riding (and thereby trampling) to the bridlepaths is a common problem although the management techniques required to gain the riders' co-operation vary considerably. In some well-used areas the waymarking of the bridlepath along the edge of a picnic area is sufficient, such as Thorndon Country Park, Essex (Plate 20). Elsewhere, physical barriers may be necessary particularly at intersections of footpaths and bridleways (Plate 21), to exclude riders from picnic areas, as described under inter-activity conflict in Chapter 11. Where horse trampling can be confined to the bridlepath network, the route can be 'sacrificial' to preserve other areas of the park or woodland. At Shotover Country Park, Oxford, the bridlepath runs beside Brazenose Wood and is heavily poached by riding, but the authorities also use the bridlepath as a 'sacrificial' route to accommodate 'fun runs' and other mass walks with high impact.

Where the bridlepaths are not rights of way, the manager has the option to close them temporarily in bad weather if they become severely poached. Where multiple routes are available, such power to close a route allows bridlepaths to be used in rotation, a technique applied at Black Park in Buckinghamshire, and Langdon Hills, Basildon. Closure of permitted routes when alternatives are not available is of limited value as riders may be determined to find a route through and trespass in the woodland as a result. At sites with permitted routes that are closed when poached, managers stress the importance of liaison to keep the riding fraternity informed, using leaflets, notices and bridleway committees, as described in Chapter 11 on inter-activity conflict.

Plate 20 — Restricting riding with waymarks is possible with a co-operative riding community . . .

Plate 21 — . . . elsewhere fences and stiles are needed.

This liaison is particularly necessary as an urban-fringe wood is often only part of the ride, so closing a woodland bridlepath could break a regular route.

Human trampling. This is rarely a problem in woods since damage to rides is highly localized and stand penetration is not a common occurrence (as described in the section on wildlife disturbance). Path improvements to steep or wet sections can channel use and prevent stand penetration. Where woodland occupies valley sides, a high standard of path maintenance is necessary if trampling is to be minimized. In woodland adjoining housing, where children playing penetrate the stands, a series of 'rabbit track' paths result, but do not seem to affect natural regeneration. Managers of heavily-used picnic sites will experience trampling and loss of grass cover particularly on sunny sites during dry summers or at the highly localized level, such as round a focal point, where protection of soft surfaces or surfacing may be needed.

Trail-bikes. Although trail-bikes do not 'trample' as such, their impact on woodland rides can be considered along with the effects of horse and pedestrian traffic. Trail-bikes are widespread, but their incidence and numbers of riders are low, and as a result cause a very localized erosion problem. Unsupervised woods are the most vulnerable, but if rangers are introduced, the bikes move elsewhere. Various physical means of exclusion are tried, ranging from kissing gates to logs blocking a gateway, but some are not ideal. If the bikers are kept out, so too are mothers with push-chairs and invalids in wheelchairs. Secondly, barriers at entry points are only of use if the whole woodland is defensible. The Forestry Commission has recently designed some gates and stiles to overcome these problems (see Appendix 1.8.5). Regular staff visits are also favoured, with some rangers resorting to trail-bikes to catch the culprits! The alternative is to adopt a positive approach and channel use to a special site, preferably leased to a club which maintains a liability insurance in case of any accidents (see 8.6).

BMX bicycles. Currently the rage with children, these are very localized in their use of woodlands, mainly in unsupervised woods adjoining housing areas and do not create an erosion problem.

9.7 Litter

In general, litter is not a problem in urban-fringe woodlands, particularly those not used for picnicking, since the other common activities, walking, riding and playing, are not major litter generators. Many managers operate a no-bins/take-your-litter-home policy, backed up by scrupulous litter collecting so that the site always looks clean, as at Bayhurst Wood Country Park, Hillingdon. Alternatively, sites can be managed with litter bins at focal points (car parks, picnic areas and kiosks, etc.), but not along the woodland rides. Only at woods with adjoining large picnic areas is much litter generated, and that is limited to the summer season.

Refuse and abandoned vehicles. Dumping of refuse and abandoned vehicles are problems for woodland managers in the urban fringe. Both are encouraged by nocturnal vehicle access into or alongside a woodland and this should be denied with gates or fencing and banks as appropriate. Woods adjoining housing estates also have a risk of domestic hardware and garden refuse being tipped and this is best solved with a tactful approach to the householders concerned, and/or a public relations exercise using *local* volunteers to clear the refuse. Managers facing the refuse problem must follow the dirt-attracts-dirt principle (see 8.5) and clear any refuse as soon as it appears. Local councils may be able to assist by clearing heavier items and abandoned cars, using their refuse department or countryside management team (see Appendix 3.2). With persistent dumping, landowners should adopt a public relations approach and ask the local press and radio to cover the clean-up operations, to make the local people aware of the problem and that positive action is being taken.

10. RECREATION MANAGEMENT TECHNIQUES II: EFFECTS ON WOODLAND MANAGEMENT AND ADJOINING LAND USE

10.1 Woodland management: choice of silvicultural system

In the eyes of the public, much of the value of recreational woodland is as a permanent landscape feature, and this suggests some form of selection system or coppice treatment for sites where amenity considerations are paramount and require permanent tree cover. In areas where permanent tree cover is not so important, for example in the urban fringe at Black Park Country Park, Buckinghamshire, clear felling and replanting can be adopted. Felling coupes can be shaped to improve the appearance of the woodland and Crowe [17] gives detailed guidance on this. Similar care needs to be taken with coppicing, for example in Linford Wood, Milton Keynes, compartments cleared as part of the 15-year coppice cycle are screened from the main ride with a fringe of trees to retain the wooded atmosphere of the ride.

In addition to the design of felling coupes, the clear felling system can be modified for amenity reasons by lengthening the rotation of the crop beyond the normal economic age for harvesting. At Black Park for example, this is done in the plantations around the main focus of visitor activity, but elsewhere in the park the normal rotation age is applied.

10.2 Choice of species

A vocal but small lobby, which is increasing rapidly in size and influence, has argued against conifers particularly in the uplands, but the attitude of the lowland woodland visitor is more equivocal [18], and the key message is the importance of variety in species, age and planting layout. It would seem that the species composition of an urban-fringe woodland is less important to the visitor than its potential as a recreation resource. Certainly conifer woods in the urban fringe like Black Park are very well used for recreation, as shown by its million annual visitors. In terms of activity *requirements*, the species composition of a woodland is of less significance than other attributes such as open areas and soil type (see 7.2 On-site factors). Selection of species, however, is ultimately the manager's choice in the light of the prescribed functions for the wood, the life of the stand, and dictates of the site. Where amenity or recreation are the principal role of the woodland, more emphasis should be given to planting larch and hardwoods where possible, even if the latter are under a conifer nurse crop. The economic attraction of planting broadleaves in recreational woodland could improve, should grants become more favourable, as currently under discussion (see Appendix 4.1.7).

10.3 Establishment of trees

Young plantations and particularly seedlings from natural regeneration are vulnerable to trampling and fire, as described in the previous chapter on environmental impact. Except in very heavily used sites such as unsupervised woods adjoining housing estates, managers need to provide only token protection for areas where young trees are being established. In Linford Wood, Milton Keynes, fencing areas of new planting has been discontinued as being unnecessary. Only a single-pole gate is sufficient to exclude the 'co-operative majority' from the young plantations at Black Park, Buckinghamshire (Plate 22). Signs explaining the need to protect young trees can also be beneficial.

Plate 22 — A single-pole gate is sufficient to exclude the co-operative majority.

In selection forestry, where young trees are planted either in small groups or individually, or are established by natural regeneration, exclusion with physical barriers is less practical because of the small scattered areas involved and only token barriers are needed. Natural barriers like brambles can be encouraged as a modest deterrent beside the woodland rides in areas where natural regeneration is occurring.

10.4 Maintenance of woodland

Of the maintenance tasks in woodland, brashing (i.e. removing dead side branches to a height of about 2 m) has some bearing on recreational woodland, particularly conifer plantations. The use of brash to discourage access into parts of the woodland important for wildlife, or reduce fire hazard has been discussed in Chapter 9 on environmental impact. Where needed, brashing can also improve access and visual penetration of the plantation edges.

Pruning and tree surgery are also maintenance operations of particular relevance to recreation. Woodland managers should prune dead and dying branches of trees alongside woodland rides, paths and car parks as a precaution against branches injuring the public. The GLC does this in its wooded urban parks like Oxleas and Abbey Woods, and its country parks like Hainault Forest and Trent Park. In a picnic area or campsite, tree surgery may be regularly needed on mature trees scattered through the site. In woodland used for riding, tree surgery is also important on bridle-paths to give sufficient height clearance for riders (see also 8.6 Insurance).

The branch-shedding danger is exacerbated by widespread public access under mature tree canopy away from rides and tracks, particularly where over-mature pollards result in a high incidence of branch shedding. Dry weather over a prolonged period, such as the dry summer of 1984, can hasten shedding and managers should post warning notices.

10.5 Thinning and extraction

This process of removing dead or suppressed trees to allow room for more vigorous trees to grow is particularly important for plantations and in restoring derelict woodland or coppice. Whereas traditional forestry methods involved the removal of dead trees from plantations, many managers now leave them *in situ* or fell them and leave the timber on the ground, for the benefit of wild-life and fungi.

Where the public is sensitive to tree felling, foresters managing recreational woods should go to considerable lengths to explain the reasons to the public. For example, prior to thinning the manager can discuss the work and the reasons for it with local environmental groups, write newspaper articles, erect notices on site and give out leaflets to the public. At Black Park, Buckingham-shire, where thinning the commercial plantations is a regular occurrence, the manager posts notices at all entry points explain-ing the purpose of forest thinning and showing which plantations are affected. Warning signs should be placed on the rides adjacent to the compartments being thinned, but no steps to exclude the public from the working area are needed.

Thinning can be used as a means of increasing the visual amenity of a woodland, for example middle-aged plantations can be given a heavy thinning to permit more shapely crowns to develop on the remaining trees. Heavy thinning can increase the light reaching the forest floor and can be applied to encourage a diverse ground flora to develop that is attractive to both visitors and wildlife. Similarly, managers can thin sycamore in their woods, because it is such an invasive species which casts a heavy shade and suppresses the ground flora which many visitors find attractive.

Timber extraction after thinning can churn up the forest floor, and should ideally take place when the ground is dry or frozen. To avoid public complaints in amenity areas, managers should consider using extraction techniques which minimize the disturbance to the woodland floor, such as forwarders, cable cranes, or light vehicles like dumptrucks. Timber extraction and thinning should be avoided at peak visitor times and particularly in heavily used areas, as there are risks of injury to the public with certain oper-ations such as felling. Alternative extraction routes can be used to avoid recreation areas or popular walks.

Although commercial demands now often dictate that timber is taken at any time of year, the ideal thinning and felling season is from November to March, outside the visitor high season. Similarly, the cutting of coppice is restricted to the dormant season when visitors happen to be fewer. These winter months are the normal times of maintenance and repair for both the forester and the park manager in the urban-fringe woodlands used for recreation.

Adjusting the work programme to avoid peak areas and times is not difficult where there is sufficient work to permit quiet areas to be thinned when other sites are occupied by visitors. At Black Park, Buckinghamshire, for example, where the main focus of activity is around the lake, thinning can proceed in plantations only 500 m away.

10.6 Security

Landowners with woodlands near housing areas may be familiar with the additional security measures needed to counter the petty thief and vandal, and it is a wise precaution to extend such measures to any recreational woodland. Stores have to be very secure, equipment cannot be left unattended, particularly overnight, and continuing problems of arson may result in a less than ideal stocking rate in commercial woodlands.

10.7 Effects on adjoining land uses: the problems

The 'spillover' effect of woodland recreation can be significant from woodlands adjoining rural land uses such as agriculture and forestry. In rural areas the 'spillover' problem is widespread and diverse in nature. On farmland the problem of trespass resulting in stock worrying or damage to crops is the main cause of concern. In adjoining woodland, trespass, disturbance to game and poaching are the principal complaints. In an urban situation, woodland does not affect adjoining land use. It is the receiver (rather than the generator) of 'spillover' effects, in the form of environmental impact from adventure play, vandalism, poaching and refuse dumping as described in Chapters 8 and 9.

Effects on adjoining farmland. Trespass is most common in small groups in the summer, particularly at blackberry-picking time when visitors are tempted into neighbouring fields. Stock worrying by free-running dogs can be a problem at sites where access routes follow the perimeter of the wood, but in many urban-fringe areas farming practices have been modified over the years to avoid these well-known problems. In the London Borough of Bromley, for example, no sheep and few cattle are kept, and most farmers concentrate on arable crops. With good public co-operation and a few advisory signs to keep dogs under control, cattle grazing and informal recreation can coexist, as at Weald Country Park in Essex.

Effects on adjoining woodland. In private woodland adjoining recreation sites the problems are trespass when *de facto* access has been allowed in the past, and disturbance or poaching of game birds. At Wormley Wood, Hertfordshire, a *de facto* bridlepath has been closed by the new owners, the Woodland Trust, in the interests of nature conservation to prevent trampling. This route used to continue in the adjoining wood, which is owned and managed for public recreation by Hertfordshire County Council. Both the Council and the Trust are finding it difficult to alter riders' habitual routes as many of the riders are teenage girls independent of riding establishments and use the woods infrequently.

In Symonshyde Great Wood, also in Hertfordshire, a picnic place was developed in 1983 to formalize existing *de facto* use, but access has been denied to the main part of the woodland by fencing the picnic site and blocking a footpath. It is too early to judge whether this 'hard line' policy of containment will be effective at Symonshyde, but it contrasts rather starkly with the positive approach to the problem of *de facto* use on the rest of the site.

Disturbance to game, and an increase in poaching in adjoining woodland can be problems where recreation is introduced or increased. For example, on the Castle Eden Walkway, 3 km outside Stockton-on-Tees, these problems were attributed to the improved public access that the Walkway created. Full-time wardening and the use of small signs saying 'Private Woodland. Please keep to the walkway' are minimizing the trespass and poaching problems.

The effect of site layout. The survey of woodlands revealed that certain factors have a significant effect on the scale of the 'spillover' problems. Sites which are bounded by roads have few problems as visitors are mostly contained on the site. Similarly, fewer problems are experienced in woodlands with a central focal point which concentrates visitors in the heart of the site, like the lake at Black Park Country Park, Buckinghamshire. Woodlands with peripheral access routes like Thorndon Country Park, Essex, or *de facto* links to adjoining land like Bencroft and Wormley Woods, Hertfordshire, are more prone to 'spillover' problems.

10.8 Management solutions

There are several key points to control these 'spillover' effects:

The importance of good liaison with neighbouring owners and managers, which can take material form such as the assistance with labour or materials for fencing and hedging, as well as informal occasional contract;

The value of regular patrolling particularly at peak visitor times or when neighbours' properties are more vulnerable, like hay-time or blackberry times;

The range and impact of physical barriers and signs used to minimize trespass is very wide. Fences and hedges are the common barriers but in one instance, at Thorndon Country Park, Essex, a muddy bridlepath outside a perimeter footpath was used to keep pedestrians on the footpath;

Where visitor use is lower, and public co-operation good, physical barriers need not be erected, as advisory signs are sufficient to deter access;

The unreasonable minority ignore low-key sign-posting but also regard heavier 'fortifications' as a challenge.

11. RECREATION MANAGEMENT TECHNIQUES III: INTER-ACTIVITY CONFLICT

11.1 Degrees of compatibility and zoning

To assess the compatibility between activities it is helpful to consider the problem as if one activity had been introduced into an area set aside for another, rather than merely cross-tabulate activities. By introducing activity A into the area set aside for activity B, the effects of A can be identified, and significantly these are not the same as the effects of introducing B into an A area. For example, while playing is compatible in a campsite, camping is not compatible in a play area. Secondly, there is the question of restricted access: playing is acceptable in a campsite if this is restricted to the campers, as allowing outsiders to play is not advisable for reasons of campsite security. Thirdly, activities compatible at low levels of use can conflict at more intensive levels. These effects are not revealed by a straightforward cross-tabulation.

The solution to these problems is one of zoning. For example, in the case of the common urban-fringe activities, it is essential to zone riding on designated routes and segregate the horses from other traffic, both foot and preferably cycle. Similarly, while off-road cycling and jogging are compatible with other path users in low numbers, where these activities are very popular, segregation from other path users becomes advantageous. Picnicking is best accommodated in a designated area, particularly if in large numbers, although at very low levels such as 5 groups/day, it is acceptable anywhere.

Table 11.1 lists the activities and development ideas (as discussed in Chapters 3, 4 and 5) and shows their degree of compatibility. The activities can be grouped into three degrees of compatibility:

Activities fully compatible with each other — 'compatible' column;

Activities best directed to specific areas or routes, but not denying access to others — 'zoned' column;

Activities demanding exclusive use of a site — 'exclusive zone' column.

Some activities appear in both the 'compatible' and 'zoned' columns because they are fully compatible at low levels of use, but require directing to special zones at medium to high levels of use, such as jogging and off-road cycling. A rather arbitrary figure of 15 people per hour starting the jogging or cycling routes has been adopted for the purposes of Table 11.1, but this obviously varies with site conditions. A wide fire-break used for the route could take a higher rate of use than an overgrown or muddy track.

All the activities listed in the 'compatible' column of Table 11.1 are mutually compatible at the specified level of use, or development in the case of the woodland restaurant. Activities best directed to specific areas or routes are listed under 'zoned' in Table 11.1 and by definition are not compatible with each other at their specified level of use. However, these zoned activities can accept the activities listed in the 'compatible' column. For example, a jogging circuit with medium to high use can accommodate walkers, dog walkers, children playing, casual wildlife observation, etc. Three of the zoned activities, riding, serious wildlife observation and off-road cycling, are however more sensitive and can only accept low levels of use from the compatible group. In addition, both riding and off-road cycle routes are obviously unsuitable as paths for the elderly or disabled, for safety reasons.

Table 11.1 — Compatibility of woodland activities and levels of use

Activity/development	Compatible at:	Zoned at:	Exclusive zone at:
Common activities			
Walking/dog walking	All levels		
Jogging	Low levels	Medium/high levels	
Picnicking		All levels	
Playing	All levels		
Riding		All levels	
Wildlife observation	Casual level	Serious level	
Uncommon activities			
Adventure play			All levels
Barbecuing		All levels	
Cycling: BMX			All levels
Cycling: off-road	Low levels	Medium/high levels	
Gathering fruit, etc.	All levels		
Trail-bike riding			All levels
Trim trail		All levels	
Wayfaring	All levels		
Camping			All levels
Caravanning			All levels
Field archery			All levels
Pheasant shooting			All levels
Rough shooting			All levels
Orienteering		All levels	
New ideas			
Adventure woodland			All levels
Fitness woodland			All levels
Equestrian woodland			All levels
Elderly/disabled provision	All levels		
Woodland restaurant	All levels		
Holiday woodland			All levels
Educational woodland		Excluding field experiments	Including field experiments
Interpretive woodland	All levels		
Community woodland	All levels		

The final column, 'exclusive zone', lists those activities and development ideas which demand the exclusive use of their site. The educational woodland appears in the exclusive zone column for sites where long-term field experiments are being conducted, such as mammal trapping, which demand the exclusion of the public if interference or vandalism are to be avoided. In the case of three of these activities, field archery, pheasant shooting and rough shooting, which are intermittent in their use of the site, time zoning can permit public access for other activities when the woodland is not used for these sports. Table 11.2 lists activities suitable for time zoning with field archery and shooting, which include each other. The degree of access allowable for the shared activities is also indicated in Table 11.2 as archery and rough shooting are not sensitive to disturbance, unlike a pheasant shoot, especially where bird feeding or rearing is involved.

Table 11.2 — Activities suitable for time zoning
with field archery and shooting

Activity/development	Archery/rough shooting	Pheasant shooting
Walking	Unrestricted	Rides, paths only
Dog walking	Unrestricted	Rides, paths, on leads only
Jogging	Unrestricted	Rides, paths only
Picnic/barbecue	Special zones only	Special zones only
Playing	Unrestricted	Special zones only
Riding	Special rides only	Special rides only
Wildlife observation	Unrestricted	Rides, paths only
Cycling, off-road	Special rides only	Special rides only
Gathering fruit, etc.	Unrestricted	Rides, paths only
Trim trail	Special path only	Special path only
Wayfaring	Unrestricted	Not compatible
Field archery	Unrestricted	Special zone only
Shooting	Unrestricted	Special zone only
Elderly/disabled	Unrestricted	Rides, paths only
Interpretation	Unrestricted	Rides, paths only
Education	Unrestricted	Rides, paths only

In addition to accepting public access for other activities by time zoning, some exclusive zones can accept supplementary activities on a restricted-user basis. For example, a campsite can be provided with a trim trail and an adventure play area for the

sole use of campers. Listed below are the supplementary activities
compatible in exclusive zones (EZ), on a restricted-user basis.

Adventure playground EZ
None.

Adventure woodland EZ
Walking/dog walking (low levels, paths only).

BMX Circuit EZ
None.

Trail-bike circuit EZ
None.

Campsite/caravan site EZ
Walking/dog walking (low levels, paths only), picnics/barbecues
(zoned), playing (zoned), wildlife observation (casual), gathering
fruit, etc., riding (zoned, hired horses), BMX circuit (zoned, hired
bikes), cycling off-road (zoned, hired bikes), trim trail (zoned),
wayfaring (zoned), interpretation woodland (zoned), woodland
restaurant, provision for elderly or disabled.

Fitness woodland EZ
Walking/dog walking (low levels), picnics/barbecues (zoned),
wildlife observation (casual), interpretation woodland (zoned),
woodland restaurant, provision for elderly or disabled.

Equestrian woodland EZ
Picnics/barbecues (zoned), wildlife observation (casual), campsite/
caravan site (zoned), interpretation woodland (zoned), woodland
restaurant, holiday woodland (zoned), provision for disabled riders.

Holiday woodland EZ
Walking/dog walking, playing (zoned), picnics/barbecues (zoned),
gathering fruit, etc., wildlife observation (casual and zoned serious),
jogging (zoned), riding (zoned, hired horses), adventure playground
(zoned), BMX circuit (zoned, hired bikes), off-road cycling (zoned,
hired bikes), trim trail (zoned), wayfaring (zoned), field archery
(zoned), shooting (zoned), adventure woodland (zoned), fitness
woodland (zoned), equestrian woodland (zoned), provision for
elderly and disabled, woodland restaurant, interpretation woodland (zoned), education woodland (zoned), community woodland.

Note that the holiday woodland is not considered compatible with trail-bike riding because of the noise and safety aspects, or with camping and caravanning because guests are already accommodated, but a joint enterprise of chalets and camp/caravan site could embrace both markets.

Educational woodland EZ (with field experiment sites)
Walking/dog walking, jogging (low levels), picnics/barbecues (zoned), wildlife observation (casual and serious), campsite/caravan site (zoned), field archery (time zoned), woodland restaurant/tearoom, provision for the disabled.

Two development ideas, the equestrian woodland and the fitness woodland, which demand use of an exclusive site on extensive path and rides, could accommodate other activities in the intervening stands of trees between the rides and paths. Such activities must avoid the rides and paths designated for riding or fitness activities, so the woodland edges are more appropriate because access can be independent of the designated ride network. Central stands surrounded by the designated network can be used for other activities provided that separate access is still possible and any junctions with the designated routes are clearly signed. Table 11.3 lists the activities that can be accommodated in between designated ride and path systems both at the periphery and the centre of a woodland.

Table 11.3 — Activities compatible between designated routes (DR)
for fitness and riding

Activity	Fitness/equestrian woodland
Picnics/barbecues	Special zones only
Wildlife observation	Unrestricted off DRs
Adventure play areas	Special zone only
BMX Circuit	Edge zone only
Wayfaring	Unrestricted off DRs
Camping site	Special zone only
Caravan site	Edge zone only
Field archery	Area/time zoned
Rough shooting	Unrestricted/time zoned

11.2 Practical solutions

The previous section examined the compatibility of a wide range of activities, but to date, practical experience of solving compatibility problems in the urban fringe is limited to the common activities. Of the woodland activities encountered in the urban fringe, walking, dog walking, riding, picnicking and children playing are the most common, whereas jogging and wildlife observation are minor activities. All of them use woodland rides as their main resource, except for picnicking which is concentrated in the open areas, and playing which uses both open areas and woodland stands. It might be assumed that this sharing of a common resource could lead to conflict between activities, *but woodland managers indicate this is far from the case.*

The riding conflict. The only conflict consistently reported is that between riders and pedestrians, and the following paragraphs detail the management techniques used to overcome the problem. The public report this conflict most frequently as a complaint about the impassable footpaths that riding creates in wet weather. A less common complaint is riders scaring other visitors by galloping on paths or through picnic areas and other zones not open to riding. Horse riding in woodlands, as elsewhere, is either on the basis of a right of way or a permitted path. Only with the latter does the woodland manager have the opportunity to issue riding permits and vary or even close the route. The permit system is not popular with local authorities because of the administrative and policing work it entails. However, it is used by the Forestry Commission, as at Joydens Wood, Bexley, in the London fringe, in the form of yellow discs which enable staff to identify authorized riders. The Commission also find that permit holders report unauthorized riders. The common management approach to riding conflict is to apply a combination of tactics:

> Segregate riding and pedestrian routes;
> Improve riders' behaviour, and
> Liaise with the riding community.

Segregation. As noted in Chapter 9 under environmental impact, waymarking can be sufficient to confine the majority of riders to designated routes (Plate 20) but often physical barriers to back up the waymarks are needed in areas with many individual riders

(Plate 21). Some managers have found that when waymarking bridlepaths in woodland, the low light levels and lichen growth make the Countryside Commission's recommended blue arrows inconspicuous (see Appendix 1.1.10). White or yellow horseshoe symbols routed in hardwood posts are favoured and consideration is often given to the riders' high viewpoint by having the signs 1.5 m above ground (Plate 20). Where a joint bridlepath and footpath is sometimes unavoidable, some form of surfacing and drainage becomes essential particularly on heavy soil (see Chapter 9).

Where horse trespass is a persistent problem, physical barriers can be used, particularly at intersections of bridlepaths and footpaths, or where bridlepaths skirt picnic areas. In Hainault Forest the GLC finds a single strand of wire on 0.5 m posts adequate to keep riders out of the stands, but as path junctions are unfenced riders can 'escape' on to the footpaths. Hampshire County Council solves this problem with simple post-and-rail fences 1.5 m high at intersections to keep horses on the bridlepath. A single rail at this height allows pushchairs and pedestrians to pass under easily, whilst acting as an effective horse barrier. The same design is used at Bayhurst Wood Country Park, Hillingdon, to lead horses around the edge of the picnic glades.

In conjunction with waymarking the route on site, it is advisable to produce route maps for noticeboards, or as handouts to riders.

Behaviour. Handouts can also incorporate a riding code of conduct. The following is an example used by Hampshire County Council at Upper Hamble Country Park:

Code of conduct for horse riders

— Use only riding tracks marked by horseshoe symbol and not footpaths.
— Beware when passing pedestrians who have strayed on to the riding tracks.
— Pass other riders quietly at a walk.
— Do not canter unless path is completely clear.
— Take particular care at crossing points and concealed sections.
— Do not walk on the bridlepaths unless leading a horse.
— Encourage good riding practice by your example to others.

(Source: Hampshire County Council, Recreation Department)

Speed restrictions on riding, such as limiting to walking or trotting on the site or zoning a particular section for galloping and warning pedestrians accordingly, can be used to minimize the hazard to pedestrians and the impact on the path. Occasionally, if a site is particularly crowded, it may be necessary to close the bridlepaths for public safety, a technique used again at Bayhurst Wood in the London fringe at Hillingdon, where the route is not a right of way.

The ranger's role. Where horse riding is in conflict with other activities the best solution is with a low-key approach by the rangers, both as a passive presence and in an advisory role. Considerable tact is necessary on occasions as a rider's elevated position can result in a rather domineering attitude towards both rangers and other visitors! A ranger on horseback can solve this problem, but is an expensive solution that is best kept as a last resort. The conflict with riding is often caused by ignorance and the educational approach does bring co-operation from most riders. The most difficult situation occurs where a large population of individual riders, usually teenage girls, use a woodland on such an infrequent basis that getting to know the riders and influencing their use of the wood are both very difficult, as at Wormley Wood, Hertfordshire (see 10.7).

Liaison. Where riding is generated by a few local establishments liaison is relatively straightforward and informal contact between the woodland manager and the riding school operator is sufficient. When a large riding community is involved a more formal approach is needed, such as contact with the British Horse Society local representative and circulars to advise local establishments and regular individual riders of route variation, problems or forest operations, events, and so on.

One of the most formal and successful approaches to minimizing conflict between riders and other woodland visitors is via a local bridleway committee. Such committees discuss route alterations and new connections, and act as a forum for riders and resource managers at county and district level to plan solutions to problem sites. This approach is used by woodland managers in Bromley, the Colne Valley Regional Park in West London and in Essex to co-ordinate route provision and advise the riding community of route alterations or temporary closures.

Such liaison can result not only in reduced conflict but in the design of new bridlepaths that are more satisfying for the rider. In Thorndon Country Park, for example, the bridlepath includes a hilly section at the riders' request, which the County Council would not have thought suitable had it not been suggested. The liaison through the bridlepaths committees can even lead to physical or financial assistance for new permitted routes, as is the case in the London Borough of Bromley, but this seems exceptional and most managers receive requests for new routes, rather than offers of help.

As a footnote to this section, it is worth mentioning that the only other area of visitor behaviour conflict to cause rangers and managers concern is not recreational as such, but concerns anti-social and criminal activities. These are discussed under ranger services in Chapter 8.

This concludes the main text of the book which has tried to illustrate the potential for recreation in urban-fringe woodland and give practical solutions to the problems of increased public access. The final part of the book comprises appendices which give sources of detailed advice, manpower and funding for owners and managers wishing to implement some of the ideas contained in the preceding chapters.

Part III of this book comprises technical appendices dealing with design of facilities, education and interpretation, sources of labour, grant aid, and conservation.

APPENDIX 1
SOURCES OF ADVICE FOR RECREATION DESIGN

1.1	General design advice	1.11	Wayfaring and orienteering
1.2	Jogging	1.12	Camping
1.3	Horse riding	1.13	Caravanning
1.4	Picnic areas	1.14	Chalets and cabins
1.5	Play areas	1.15	Archery
1.6	Barbecue sites	1.16	Shooting
1.7	BMX cycling	1.17	Providing for the elderly
1.8	Off-road cycling		and disabled
1.9	Trail-bike riding	1.18	Restaurant and tea room
1.10	Trim trail		

Note. Advice relating to education, interpretation and wildlife observation is given in Appendix 2, and nature conservation in Appendix 5.

1.1 General design advice

1.1.1   One of the most comprehensive sources of design advice on all aspects of countryside recreation is available from the Countryside Commission for Scotland (CCS) at Battleby. It is in the form of two ring-binders of information sheets which are regularly added to or updated, and currently costs £20, including post and packing. The contents are listed below, and the CCS may make available single information sheets for those requiring advice on a specific subject.

The Battleby Display Centre Information Sheets and Catalogue

1. Litter bins
2. Signs, notices and information boards
3. Surfacing materials
4. Barriers and fencing
5. Picnic furniture and seating
6. Footpaths, steps and walkways
7. Hides, cabins and shelters (in preparation)
8. Leaflet dispensers and talking/ listening posts (in preparation)
9. (To be announced)
10. Drainage (in preparation)
11. Toilets (in preparation)
12. Viewpoint indicators (in preparation)
13. Building finishes and materials
14. Fireplaces, barbecues, etc.
15. Vehicle management (in preparation)
16. Bridges
17. Provision for disabled people
18. Techniques, methods, etc.
19. Bibliographies, reading lists, etc.
20. Catalogue of exhibits (on display at Battleby, Perth)

Source: The Countryside Commission for Scotland, Battleby, Redgorton, Perth PH1 3EW. Telephone (0738) 27921.

1.1.2   A second source of general design advice is *Designed for Recreation* by Elizabeth Beazley. Published by Fabers, 1969, out of print. Source: Libraries.

Certain topics have received special attention, but are not associated with particular activities, so are listed here.

Footbridges

1.1.3   *Footbridges in the Countryside: Design and Construction* by Reiach Hall Blyth Partnership. For: Countryside Commission for Scotland. Source: CCS. Source: CCS (see 1.1.1). Price: £1.46 (incl. p & p).

Signs

1.1.4   *Construction and Design of Signs in the Countryside*, published by CCS. Source: CCS (see 1.1.1). Price: £1.46.

1.1.5   *Information Signs for the Countryside* CCP 132, published by the Countryside Commission (England and Wales). Source: Countryside Commission, Publications Despatch Department, 19/23 Albert Road, Manchester M19 2EQ. Telephone: (061) 224 6287. Price: £6.12 (incl. p & p).

1.1.6   *Symbols* CCP 118 (illustrates symbols for countryside recreation), published by the Countryside Commission (England and Wales). Source: CC (see 1.1.5). Price: £0.73 (incl. p & p).

Surfaces for car parks, paths, bridleways

1.1.7   *Surfaces for Rural Car Parks* CCP 45, published by the Countryside Commission (England and Wales). Source: as 1.1.5. Price: £0.52 (incl. p & p).

1.1.8   *Surfacing Materials for use on Footpaths, Cycletracks and Bridleways* CCP 66, published by the Countryside Commission (England & Wales). Out of print. Source: CC Library for Consultation, John Dower House, Crescent Place, Cheltenham GL50 3RA. Telephone: (0242) 521381, or loaned through the library service.

1.1.9   *Footpaths – A Practical Handbook* by Elizabeth Agate, for the British Trust for Conservation Volunteers. Source: BTCV, 36 St. Mary's Street, Wallingford, Oxford OX10 0EU. Telephone: (04991) 39766. Price: £9.20 (incl. p & p).

Waymarking routes

1.1.10   *Waymarking Public Paths* (includes bridleways), published by the Countryside Commission. Source: see 1.1.5. Price: Free.

Note. Some woodland managers have found the blue colour recommended for bridlepath waymarking is not clear under closed canopy conditions where light levels are low and the humidity encourages lichen growth. White or yellow horseshoes are preferred.

Personal advice

1.1.11 *Recreation Design.* Landowners throughout UK are particularly recommended to visit the display of materials and methods developed by the Countryside Commission for Scotland at Battleby outside Perth, where the Display Centre Manager, Mr M. J. Bease, can advise on particular design problems (see 1.1.1).

1.1.12 *Courses.* The *Countryside Commission* sponsors training courses with a 50% subsidy, on a variety of topics dealing with recreation design and management. Recent courses include: Countryside Management and Recreation, Marketing in Countryside Recreation, Disability and Countryside Recreation, Organization of Events, Working with Volunteers for Recently Appointed Rangers. Details of the courses can be obtained from *The Countryside Commission,* John Dower House, Crescent Place, Cheltenham GL50 3RA. Telephone: (0242) 521381.

The Countryside Commission for Scotland also runs training courses, and details can be obtained from the Education and Training Officer (see 1.1.1).

1.1.13 *The Forestry Commission* has extensive experience of woodland recreation, but is not yet able to offer a formal advisory service to landowners. At an informal level, however, local foresters in the FC may well be able to suggest solutions to a particular problem facing a woodland owner.

1.1.14 *The Tourist Boards* are able to advise on marketing aspects of recreation projects, particularly for projects with wide catchments, e.g., a caravan site. Landowners should approach their regional tourist boards via the addresses given below.

English Tourist Board, 4 Grosvenor Gardens, London SW1W 0DU. Telephone: (01) 730 3400.
Wales Tourist Board, Brunel House, 2 Fitzalan Road, Cardiff CF2 1UY. Telephone: (0222) 499909.
Scottish Tourist Board, 23 Ravelston Terrace, Edinburgh EH4 3EU. Telephone: (031) 332 2433.
North Ireland Tourist Board, River House, 48 High Street, Belfast BT1 2DS. Telephone: (0232) 231221.

The Tourist Boards also produce a series of very helpful publications, such as *Tourism Marketing for the Small Business.* Source: English Tourist Board. Price: £2.00.

1.1.15 *The Landscape Institute* is the professional body for landscape architects, managers and scientists. Landscape advice is important for any recreation project, particularly those involving buildings. The Institute operates a nominations procedure to assist landowners in the selection of a consultant most suited to their particular requirements. Landowners should contact the Registrar at the following address: The Landscape Institute, 12 Carlton House Terrace, London SW1Y 5AH. Telephone: (01) 839 4044.

Planning permission

1.1.16   Landowners are strongly recommended to have early discussions about their proposals with the local planning authority. The English Tourist Board (ETB) has produced a helpful guide on this subject entitled *Obtaining Planning Permission*. Source: ETB (see 1.1.14). Price: £1.50.

Advice relating to specific activities follows.

1.2 Jogging

1.2.1   Being a relatively new sport there is no published information specific to jogging. Jogging circuits require soft, well-drained surfaces of soil, hoggin, or wood chippings, with the opportunity to vary the route. Routes need not be segregated from other activities, with the exception of muddy horse rides and bridleways which are not suitable. Specially designated routes are not necessary as joggers running several times a week like to have a variety of routes to use, so a network of woodland rides and paths is preferred.

1.2.2   Owners can obtain further advice from the national body or their local jogging club which would be very pleased to advise on provision, and can be contacted via The National Jogging Association, Newstead Abbey Park, Newstead, Nottinghamshire. Telephone: (0623) 793496.

1.2.3   *Surfacing materials for use on footpaths cycletracks and bridleways*. Source: see 1.1.8.

1.2.4   *Trim Trails — A Guide to their Design and Use*, p. 5. Source: see 1.10.1.

1.3 Horse riding

1.3.1   *Facilities for Recreational Riding*, published by the British Horse Society. Source: BHS, British Equestrian Centre, Stoneleigh, Kenilworth, Warwickshire CV8 2LR. Telephone: (0203) 52241. Price: Free.

1.3.2   *Policy Statement on Width of Bridleways*, published by the BHS. Source: as above. Price: Free.

1.3.3   Woodland owners are advised to discuss any riding proposals with the local BHS representative who can be found via the National HQ, see 1.3.1 above.

1.3.4   *The Hertfordshire Bridleways Project*, published by Hertfordshire County Council (due late 1984). Source: Hertfordshire Countryside Officer,

County Planning Department, County Hall, Hertford SG13 8DN. Telephone: (0992) 54242.

1.3.5   *Surfacing Materials for use on footpaths, cycletracks and bridleways.* Source: see 1.1.8.

1.4 Picnic areas

1.4.1   *Battleby Catalogue*, Section 5. Source: see 1.1.1.

1.4.2   *Designed for Recreation*, Chapter 7. Source: see 1.1.2.

1.5 Play areas

1.5.1   *Designed for Recreation*, p. 130. Source: see 1.1.2.

1.5.2   *Providing for Children's Play in the Countryside*, 1984, by Timothy Cochrane Associates for Countryside Commission for Scotland and Forestry Commission. Source: CCS (as 1.1.1). Price: £7.63 (incl. p & p).

1.5.3   *Playground Management for Local Councils*, 1983, by National Playing Fields Association. Source: NPFA, 25 Ovington Square, London SW3 1LQ. Price: £3.95 (incl. p & p).

1.5.4   *The Play Board* has been established recently to promote facilities for children's play. The Board is able to provide general advice on the design and layout of facilities, and is preparing a series of fact sheets; current titles include finance, safety and insurance. Landowners interested in providing for children's play are recommended to contact the Board for advice at the following address: The Play Board, Britannia House, 50 Great Charles Street, Birmingham B3 24P. Telephone: (021) 233 3399.

1.6 Barbecue sites

1.6.1   *Battleby Catalogue*, Sections 5 and 14. Source: see 1.1.1.

1.6.2   *Designed for Recreation*, Chapter 7. Source: see 1.1.2.

1.6.3   *Forestry Practice*, Chapter 7, Fire. Forestry Commission Bulletin 14. Source: HMSO Bookshops. Price: £3.50.

1.7 BMX cycling

1.7.1   Design advice on practice circuits is available from: UK-BMX, 5 Church Hill, Staplehurst, Tonbridge, Kent TN12 0AY. Telephone: (0580) 892803.

1.7.2   UK-BMX also provide a design guide to the construction of standard competition courses, and a construction service.

1.8 Off-road cycling

With the novelty of this pursuit, little has been written specifically about designing trails for off-road cycling, but useful information is available in the section dealing with footpaths and tracks in the following:

1.8.1   *Battleby Catalogue*, Sections 3, 4, 6 and 16. Source: see 1.1.1.

1.8.2   *Footbridges in the Countryside*. Source: see 1.1.3.

1.8.3   *Surfacing materials for use on footpaths, cycletracks and bridleways*. Source: see 1.1.8.

1.8.4   *Footpaths – a practical handbook*. Source: see 1.1.9.

1.8.5   Route selection criteria, a forest cycling code and designs of gates and stiles to permit bicycle access but exclude motorbikes and horses, are available from the Forestry Commission, upon written request to: Design and Recreation Branch, Forestry Commission, 231 Corstorphine Road, Edinburgh EH12 7AT.

1.9 Trail-bike riding

1.9.1   Woodland owners experiencing unauthorized trail-bike riding or wanting advice on design of facilities should approach ACU headquarters in the first instance, to be put in touch with ACU regional staff: Auto-Cycle Union, Millbuck House, Corporation Street, Rugby CV21 2DN. Telephone: (0788) 70332.

1.9.2   See also 1.8.5 above for designs of gates and stiles.

1.10 Trim trail

1.10.1   *Trim Trails – A Guide to their Design and Use*, published by the Sports Council. Source: The SC Publications Unit, 16 Upper Woburn Place, London WC1H 0QP. Telephone: (01) 388 1277. Price: £1.00.

The following contain useful advise about constructing and improving paths.

1.10.2   *Surfacing materials for use on footpaths, cycletracks and bridleways*. Source: see 1.1.8.

1.10.3   *Footpaths – a practical handbook*. Source: see 1.1.9.

1.11 Wayfaring and orienteering

1.11.1   *Creating New Wayfaring Schemes and Permanent O-Courses*, published by the British Orienteering Federation. Source: BOF, 41 Dale Road, Matlock, Derbyshire DE4 3LT. Telephone: (0629) 3661. Price: Free.

1.11.2   *What is Wayfaring?* Published by the Forestry Commission. Source: BOF (see 1.11.1). Price: Free.

1.12 Camping

1.12.1   *Designed for Recreation*, Chapter 8. Source: see 1.1.2.

1.12.2   Youth Groups. As there is no national co-ordinating body, woodland owners interested in providing a site for youth groups should contact local organizations or their national headquarters, e.g.:

The Scout Association, Baden-Powell House, 65 Queen's Gate, London SW7. Telephone: (01) 584 7030.
The Girl Guides Association, 17–19 Buckingham Palace Road, London SW1. Telephone: (01) 834 6242.
The Boy's Brigade, The Girl's Brigade, Brigade House, Parsons Green, London shire CV8 2LG. Telephone: (0203) 23507.

1.12.3   Tourist camping. Woodland owners interested in providing a site for tourist camping should obtain a copy of *Developing a Touring, Camping or Caravan Site*, published by the English Tourist Board. Source: see 1.1.14. Price: £1.50.
The National Federation of Site Operators (NFSO) is pleased to advise landowners about establishing a commercial campsite: NFSO, Chichester House, 31 Park Road, Gloucester GL1 1LH. Telephone: (0452) 26911.
The Camping Club would also be pleased to advise landowners about establishing a club campsite: The Camping and Caravanning Club, 11 Lower Grosvenor Place, London SW1W 0EY. Telephone: (01) 828 1012.

1.13 Caravanning

1.13.1   Guidance for woodland owners interested in providing caravan sites, either small 'certificated locations' or larger more equipped sites, is contained in *Developing a Touring, Camping or Caravan Site* (see 1.12.3 above). The NFSO (see 1.12.3) or either of the clubs below will be pleased to advise on site suitability and caravanning requirements.

The Caravan Club, East Grinstead House, East Grinstead, West Sussex RH19 1UA. Telephone: (0342) 26944.
The Camping and Caravanning Club, 11 Lower Grosvenor Place, London SW1W 0EY. Telephone: (01) 828 1012.

1.13.2   *Designed for Recreation*, Chapter 8. Source: see 1.1.2.

1.13.3   *Caravan Sites and Control of Development Act*, 1960. Circular 28/83 (revised 1983). Published by the Department of the Environment. Source: HMSO. Price: £1.40.

1.14 Chalets and cabins

1.14.1 The NFSO (see 1.12.3) would be pleased to advise landowners interested in a chalet or cabin development.

1.14.2 *Purpose Built Chalets and Cabins* (survey of costs and specifications of chalets and cabins available in UK, published 1982 by the English Tourist Board). Source: ETB (see 1.1.14). Price: £5.50.

1.14.3 *Holiday Home Development – Timesharing.* Source: English Tourist Board (see 1.1.14). Price: £3.00.

1.14.4 *Forestry Commission Potential for Permanent Tourist Accommodation,* 1974 (an interesting, if now dated, assessment). Source: Forestry Commission Publications, Alice Holt Lodge, Wrecclesham, Farnham, Surrey GU10 4LH. Price: £2.00.

1.15 Archery

1.15.1 Woodland owners interested in leasing a site to a field archery club should approach the national organisation: The Grand National Archery Society, The National Agricultural Centre, Stoneleigh, Kenilworth, Warwickshire CV8 2LG. Telephone: (0203) 23507.

1.16 Shooting

1.16.1 The Game Conservancy (GC) offers advice by letter, over the 'phone or in person on all aspects of game management: The Game Conservancy, Fordingbridge, Hampshire SP6 1EF. Telephone: (0425) 53281.

1.16.2 *Woodlands for Pheasants,* published by GC. Source: GC (see 1.16.1 above). Price: £3.00 (incl. p & p).

1.16.3 The Game Conservancy also runs courses for owners and keepers on aspects of game management.

1.16.4 The British Association for Shooting and Conservation (BASC) offers advice to members and the public on game management, by literature and in person: The BASC, Masford Mill, Rossett, Wrexham, Clwyd LL12 0HL. Telephone: (0244) 570881.

1.17 Providing for the elderly and disabled

1.17.1 *Battleby Catalogue,* Section 17. Source: see 1.1.1.

1.17.2 *Informal Recreation for Disabled People.* Countryside Commission Advisory Series No. 15. Source: as 1.1.5. Price: Free.

1.18 Restaurant or tea room

1.18.1 *How to start a Small Restaurant or Tea Room.* Source: English Tourist Board (see 1.1.14). Price: £1.50.

APPENDIX 2
EDUCATION AND INTERPRETATION

2.1   Themes and ideas.
2.2   Sources of advice.
2.3   Sources of materials.

2.1 Themes and ideas

The woodland owner has a great opportunity to fill the vacuum in public understanding about the importance of woodland and forestry. Outlined below are some woodland themes which could be developed for education and interpretation together with some ideas on methods more suited to the urban-fringe site.

Themes

2.1.1   A walk round the woodland linking age, size and value of the tree to stages of the management cycle. Show how the natural vegetation changes with the forest cycle.

2.1.2   Traditional forest methods linked to a history of the site, who worked it and for what products; use the 'oral tradition' of elderly local inhabitants or woodsmen recalling 'how it was in my day, my grandfather's day'.

2.1.3   The value of woodland in the landscape for screening, making dramatic viewpoints, etc. The slow growth and apparent unchanging character of woodland, the problems the slow growth gives in relation to changing demands for timber.

2.1.4   Timber uses, the properties of timbers related to their uses, especially everyday articles. Seeing, feeling and smelling samples of timber. The skill of old woodcrafts in selecting trees for different purposes.

2.1.5   The height of a tree, its volume of timber and value, its rate of growth, how it is cut, the values of different timbers, the value of the whole woodland, the time-scale of production in relation to changing markets.

2.1.6   The special nature of the woodland environment, its micro-climate which provides the only habitat for organisms A, B, C, etc.; its longevity and lack of disturbance in relation to specialist organisms, the idea of ancient woodland being particularly important for conservation, the life in the canopy, trunk space, on the ground and in the soil. The idea of natural regeneration, woodland succession, tree reproduction in relation to the role of man in destroying and conserving woodland.

2.1.7   Tree identification, how to tell A from B in summer, and a similar theme repeated in winter. Involving the visitor feeling bark and leaves, smelling flowers, sap and resins, collecting a leaf or a twig in a polythene bag, learning how to press leaves. What trees prefer which conditions.

Ideas and methods

2.1.8   The basic problem is how to interest the regular visitor, to whet his appetite to come back to find out more on future occasions. The approaches used must involve the visitor in activity and ideally requires an 'interpreter' on site, rather than rely on the passive distribution of information from a leaflet dispenser, or static display. Some ideas on methods more suited to urban-fringe conditions are given below.

2.1.9   *The guided walk.* In small groups these are some of the best ways of getting the message across as the guide (interpreter) can adjust the message to the level and areas of interest shown by the group. When walks are arranged with specific groups in advance, the levels and areas of interest can be more clearly defined. Alternatively, an *ad hoc* group can assemble at an appointed time, and attract a wider audience. Thirdly, such walks can be linked to specific events, see 2.1.10.

2.1.10   *Open days/events.* In the urban fringe where short duration trips are more normal, a permanent interpretive presence may be less appropriate. Alternatively, open days or events can be staged involving a series of attractions, e.g., guided walks, demonstrations of old woodland crafts linked to sales of woodland produce, aimed especially at the householder and gardener; nature weeks with temporary nature trails; tree-canopy trails on scaffolding; try-your-hand-at-forestry events and training volunteer management crews.

2.1.11   *The simple visitor centre: a nature hut.* A simple information point which can be manned at the busy periods to provide information services, e.g., identify specimens or 'reported sightings', provide reference books, charts and specimens for public consultation. It can also provide topical information about what can be seen in the woodland this month, week or even today, provide information about other woodlands and places of interest in the locality which may appeal to the clientele; answer any questions about current woodland management operations or policy issues. The information centre can also promote public involvement by providing polythene bags for collecting leaves and twigs and even venture into selling a few guide books for tree and bird identification, etc.

2.1.12   *The labelled walk.* An unstructured nature trail in effect, with items of interest identified and explained throughout the woodland or along a specific route, for the visitors to read or not, as they please. This is more suited to the urban fringe than the standard nature-trail leaflet method as it can reach a wider audience by including those who would not think of buying/obtaining a leaflet. The labelled walk may also reach the regular visitor as the material is always on display, like the more sophisticated display walk (see 2.1.13). Simple production can be by stencil inside polythene bags which have the advantage of easy replacement if vandalized, or to change the content.

2.1.13   *The display walk.* This is a nature trail with the leaflet replaced by a series of trailside display panels or exhibits. It has the same advantages for urban-fringe use over the leaflet method as the labelled walk, but is more expensive to create, and replace when vandalized or when the content is to be changed. It also shares the same disadvantage of relying on the written word to spread the message, which has limited appeal.

2.2 Sources of advice

2.2.1   *Centre for Environmental Interpretation*, Manchester Polytechnic, John Dalton Building, Chester Street, Manchester M1 5GD. Telephone: (061) 228 6171.

The Centre for Environmental Interpretation (CEI), Manchester Polytechnic, is a national centre with a brief to promote environmental interpretation through training and advice in its principles and techniques. CEI operates in three main areas, all of which are closely related: training; information and advice; research and consultancy. It is supported by grant aid from the Carnegie Trust. CEI can provide support in the following areas:

- advice by phone or letter on the planning and implementation of interpretation projects, including sources of grant aid;
- reading list of woodland owners considering interpretation projects;
- consultancy service for the planning and implementation of specific interpretation projects;
- training courses, workshops and seminars on all aspects of planning and managing interpretive services.

Landowners wishing to use the CEI services should contact either of the Co-Directors, Gillian Binks or Graham Barrow, at the address above.

2.2.2   *Council for Environmental Education*, School of Education, University of Reading, Reading RG1 4RU. Telephone: (0734) 875234.

The CEE maintains a list of environmental education advisers in Local Education Authorities and landowners are recommended to approach the advisers when considering the educational use of their woodland.

2.2.3   *Nature Conservancy Council*, through its regional offices, can give advice on the aspects of a site's natural history which may be suitable for interpretation. The regional offices may be found in the telephone directory or through headquarters: The Nature Conservancy Council, Northminster House, Peterborough PE1 1UA. Telephone: (09733) 40345.

2.2.4   *The county conservation trusts* will be able to advise on the natural history aspects of a site, worthy of interpretation. County trusts may be found in the telephone directory or via their national organization: Royal Society for Nature Conservation, The Green, Nettleham, Lincoln LN2 2NR. Telephone: (0522) 752326.

Courses

2.2.5   *The Countryside Commission* sponsors training courses with a 50% subsidy on a variety of topics in the field of interpretation. Recent courses include: education in the countryside; countryside interpretation; audio-visual aids in interpretation; design and graphics in interpretation. Details of the courses are available from The Countryside Commission, John Dower House, Crescent Place, Cheltenham GL50 3RA. Telephone: (0242) 521381.

2.2.6   *The Countryside Commission for Scotland* also runs training courses on interpretation subjects, and Scottish residents only pay for accommodation; others pay also for tuition. Details of the courses are available from The Countryside Commission for Scotland, Battleby, Redgorton, Perth PH1 3EW. Telephone: (0738) 27921.

Publications giving guidance on interpretation

2.2.7   *Guide to Countryside Interpretation — Part I Principles of Countryside Interpretation and Interpretive Planning. Part II Interpretive Media and Facilities.* Published by HMSO, 1975, for the Countryside Commissions. Source: HMSO bookshops and Countryside Commission, Publications Despatch Department, 19/23 Albert Road, Manchester M19 2EQ. Telephone: (061) 224 6287. Price: Part I £1.51 (incl. p & p); Part II £4.27 (incl. p & p).

2.2.8   *Countryside Commission Advisory Series: No. 2 Interpretive Planning. No. 4 Guided Walks. No. 9 Self-guided Trails.* The following show how farms are being opened to the public but may give guidance to woodland owners: *No. 3 Farm Open Days. No. 14 The Public on the Farm.* Source: CC (as 2.2.7 above), free of charge.

2.2.9   *The Countryside on View* by Elizabeth Beazley, published by Constable, 1971 (out of print). Source: Libraries.

Designs for wildlife observation hides

2.2.10   *Battleby Catalogue*, Section 7 (in preparation). Source: see Appendix 1.1.1.

2.2.11   *Designed for Recreation*, Chapter 12. Source: see Appendix 1.1.2.

2.2.12   *Informal Countryside Recreation for Disabled People*, page 56. Source: see Appendix 1.17.2.

2.2.13   The RSPB can provide information and advice on the design and siting of birdwatching hides, which is available from The Reserves Department,

Royal Society for the Protection of Birds, The Lodge, Sandy, Bedfordshire SG19 2DL. Telephone: (0767) 80551.

2.2.14 Mr Malcolm Fisher has recently completed some designs for hides which have been published in *Parks* magazine, in a brief form: 'The Wildlife Observation Hide' in *Parks* 9(2) July–September 1984, pages 17–19. *Parks* can be consulted at the Countryside Commission (see 2.2.5). Mr Fisher is hoping to publish more detailed versions of his hides elsewhere and he can be contacted for further details at: 23 Summerleys, Eaton Bray, Near Dunstable, Bedfordshire. Telephone: (0707) 44660, ext. 39.

2.3 Sources of materials

The following organizations supply posters and other off-the-shelf educational materials that might be of use as a first step towards interpretation and education, e.g., explanatory posters about woodland wildlife.

2.3.1 *British Museum (Natural History)*, Cromwell Road, London SW7. Telephone: (01) 589 6323.

Wallchart: *Deciduous Woodland* 24 × 31 ins. Colour, illustrates the plant life of a deciduous wood. Price: £0.75.

Wallchart: *Scottish Pine Forests* 24 × 31 ins. Colour, illustrates the plant life of a native pine wood. Price: £0.75.

2.3.2 *Conservation Trust*, c/o George Palmer School, Northumberland Avenue, Reading RG2 0EN. Telephone: (0734) 868442.

Study Notes − Trees (1980) 6 pages. For use by teachers in lesson preparation and by pupils in project work, etc. A4, illustrated. Price: £0.30.

Study Kit − Look at that Tree. An all-subject approach for 11–14 yrs. pupils. Price: £0.75.

Study Pack − Tree Pack. Contains a selection of material produced by the Trust and others; includes notes, leaflets, posters and booklets. Price: £1.50.

Environmental Education Enquiries by Peter Berry, 22 pages, A4. Details of over 250 environmental organizations and the help they give. Price: £0.50.

Guide to Resources in Environmental Education by Peter Berry. 84 pages. Comprehensive listings of kits, filmstrips, books, posters, etc., classified by subject. Price: £1.50.

Display Pack − Trees. Six assorted coloured posters and back-up material *for hire per month*. Price: £2.50. The Trust can also arrange exhibitions for a fee.

In addition to the items listed above for sale or hire, the Trust operates a 'Resource Bank' from which members may borrow materials and equipment. Initial registration costs £15.00 with £1.00 annual subscription for the newsletter, and woodland owners are eligible for membership.

2.3.3 *Countryside Commission*, Publications Despatch Department, 19/23 Albert Road, Manchester M19 2EQ. Telephone: (061) 224 6287.

Poster: *Waymarking — keeps you on the right track* 420 × 297 mm, colour. Price: Free.

2.3.4 *Forestry Commission*, Publications Section, Alice Holt Lodge, Wrecclesham, Farnham, Surrey GU10 4LH. Telephone: (0420) 22255.

Teachers Handbook. Guide to resource materials, project themes and general information about visiting woodland. Price: Free.

Leaflet: *A brief guide to Britain's principal trees.* A short introduction to trees and their timber. Price: Free.

Wallchart: *The working forest* 540 × 890 mm, b/w for colouring. Price: £0.10.

Wallchart: *The living forest* 540 × 890 mm, coloured. Illustrates the changing wildlife of a commercial upland forest and the FC's conservation measures. Price: £0.20.

Wallchart: *Timber in Britain.* Price: £0.10.

Poster: *Fire posters* — supplied for display purposes, warning of the dangers of fire to woodlands. Price: Free.

Map: *Forestry in Britain* 380 × 305 mm. Map of all forests in Britain, FC boundaries and offices. Free.

Wallcharts: *Forest trees* 520 × 820 mm. Identification charts showing leaves, fruit, flowers, bark and tree for: 1. Oak; 2. Birch; 3. Scots Pine; 4. Douglas Fir; 5. Beech; 6. Elm; 7. European Larch; 8. Sitka Spruce; 9. Sycamore; 10. Corsican Pine; 11. Ash; 12. Lime; 13. Norway Spruce; 14. Sweet Chestnut. Price: £0.60 each or £8.50 set.

2.3.5 *Nature Conservancy Council*, Interpretive Branch, Northminster House, Peterborough PE1 1UA. Telephone: (0733) 40345.

Cardboard woodland 80 cm × 120 cm tall, 60 cm deep. Introduces oak wood ecology to children. Slot-together model. Price: £6.00.

Wallchart: *Wildlife, the Law and You* 840 × 550 mm. Illustrates some of the species protected under the *Wildlife and Countryside Act* 1981. Price: £1.00.

Wallchart: *Oak woods* 840 × 39 mm. Illustrates the habitat and some of its wildlife. Price: £1.00.

Booklet: *Conservation of semi-natural upland woodland.* 12 pages, A5. Price: £0.30.

Booklet: *Conservation of lowland broadleaf woodland.* 12 pages, A5. Price: £0.30.

Booklet: *Why plant native broadleaf trees.* 8 pages, A5. Price: £0.20.

2.3.6 *Pictorial Charts Educational Trust*, 27 Kirchen Road, London W13. Telephone: (01) 567 5343.

Wallchart: *The Ecology of an Oak Tree* 760 × 1015 mm. Colour, illustrating food web round an oak tree. Price: £3.40.

Wallchart: *Cold Temperate Lands* 730 × 1015 mm. Colour, illustrating the industries and wildlife in conifer forest. Price: £3.40.

2.3.7 *Royal Society for Nature Conservation*, The Green, Nettleham, Lincoln LN2 2NR. Telephone: (0522) 752326.

WATCH Outdoor Guide: *Woods*, 32 pages, colour, ideas and ways of exploring nature. Price: £1.00.

Habitat model: *Woodland* 12 × 8 × 10 ins., accompanied by teacher's notes, slot-together model, to colour. Price: £2.25.

Wallchart: *Broadleaved Woodland* 34 × 22 ins. Illustrates the habitat and some of its wildlife. Price: £1.50.

Book: *Discovering the Countryside with David Bellamy — Woodland Walks*. Price: £4.95.

WATCH Project Pack: *Tree Kit*, includes booklets, tree planting game and wallchart. Price: £2.50.

2.3.8 *Royal Society for the Prevention of Accidents*, Cannon House, The Priory Queensway, Birmingham B4 6BS. Telephone: (021) 233 2461.

Poster: *These fruits are dangerous* 30 × 20 ins. Text and identification drawings of fruits in colour. Price: £0.60.

Poster: *Poisonous fungi* 30 × 20 ins. Text and identification drawings of fungi in colour. Price: £0.60.

2.3.9 *Royal Society for the Protection of Birds*, The Lodge, Sandy, Bedfordshire SG19 2DL. Telephone: (0767) 80551.

Poster: *If you go down to the woods today* 420 × 594 mm. Colour, illustrating some wildlife of broadleaved and coniferous woods in winter and summer. Price: postage only.

2.3.10 *Timber Research and Development Association*, Stocking Lane, Hughenden Valley, High Wycombe, Buckinghamshire HP14 4ND. Telephone: (024024) 2771.

Wallcharts dealing with wood technology, to be reprinted in 1985, covering: how a tree grows; timber structure; drying of wood and moisture content (4 wallcharts). Price to be announced.

2.3.11 *Tree Council*, Agriculture house, Knightsbridge, London SW1X 7NJ. Telephone: (01) 235 8554.

Poster: *Trees of Britain*, 45 species, deciduous and coniferous, summer and winter outlines, leaf-shape. 410 × 584 mm. Price: £0.50.

Games Pack: Happy Families, a mobile and other games. Price: £1.25.

2.3.12 *Urban Spaces Scheme*, Department of Food and Biological Sciences, Polytechnic of North London, Holloway, London N7 8DB. Telephone: (01) 607 2789.

Book: *Trees and Urban Areas*, 77 pages, A4. Price: £3.00.

Book: *Leaf Litter and Decomposition*, in preparation.

2.3.13   *Woodland Trust*, Westgate, Grantham, Lincolnshire NG31 6LL. Telephone: (0476) 74297.

Wallchart: *Pictorial Guide to Common Woodland Trees*, showing trees summer and winter, foliage and fruits. 24 × 36 ins. Price: £1.50.

Tape: *A Walk in Pontburn Wood with David Bellamy*, how to appreciate woodlands, the role of the WT and its management work. Price: £4.95.

Book: *Out of the Wood*, hbk., 22 pages, Oxford University Press. The story of the life and times of an oak tree over 900 years. 16 pages of illustrations. For children. Price: £5.95.

2.3.14   *Educational Productions*. This firm has been recently taken over by A & C Black, and their series of wallcharts on forest trees has been discontinued.

APPENDIX 3
SOURCES OF LABOUR

3.1   Community woodland and woodcraft training
3.2   Countryside management schemes
3.3   Manpower Services Commission community programmes.
3.4   Military aid to the civil community

3.1 Community woodland and woodcraft training

3.1.1   *The Woodland Trust* has been running a successful community woodland project outside Bromsgrove and is preparing a report on the scheme in the form of a 'resource pack' to assist landowners wishing to set up similar projects. Landowners interested in the community woodland approach should contact the project officer: Mr Andrew Thompson, 4 Church Road, Catshill, Bromsgrove, Worcestershire. Telephone: (0527) 35448; or the Woodland Trust headquarters: The Woodland Trust, Westgate, Grantham, Lincolnshire NG31 6LL. Telephone: (0476) 74297.

3.1.2   *The British Trust for Conservation Volunteers* runs courses to train volunteers and leaders, organizes tasks for volunteers to carry out, and produces useful technical publications. Conservation volunteers can assist the woodland owner in the following ways:

1. Running demonstrations/events to attract interest in woodland management and other conservation tasks.
2. Training volunteers in woodland crafts, skills in hand-tools and team management (this can be combined with a management task in the owner's woodland).

3. Carrying out woodland management and other conservation tasks, e.g., restoring derelict coppice, fencing a bridleway, removing household refuse, in the owner's woodland.

Conservation Volunteers have a national headquarters for England, Wales and Northern Ireland at: 36 St. Mary's Street, Wallingford, Oxfordshire OX10 0EU. Telephone: (0491) 39766. Scotland has a separate organization: Scottish Conservation Projects, 70 Main Street, Doune, Perthshire FK16 6BW. Telephone: (0786) 841479.

Publications

3.1.3 *Conservation Volunteers* produce a book on organizing volunteers and a series of very detailed handbooks on aspects of practical management, which are available from their headquarters (see 3.1.2).

Developing skills with conservation volunteers. Free. (Annual programme of training events.)

Organising a local conservation group. Price: £1.60.

Conservation Handbook Series: *Woodlands* £8.40; *Footpaths* £9.20; *Hedging* £6.30; *Dry Stone Walling* £6.30; *Fencing* (to be published Autumn 1985).

3.1.4 *Volunteers in the Countryside.* Countryside Commission Advisory Series No. 11. Source: Countryside Commission, Publications Despatch Department, 19/23 Albert Road, Manchester M19 2EP. Telephone: (061) 224 6287. Price: Free.

3.2 Countryside management schemes

3.2.1 *The Countryside Commission* has been sponsoring countryside management schemes in various parts of the country, e.g., Hertfordshire, and more recently through the Groundwork Trusts in the north-west, e.g., St. Helens. The underlying approach of these schemes is to improve the landscape and access to it, by small-scale public works projects on public and private land, e.g., bridleway improvement, fencing woodland to exclude stock or motorbikes. The projects are carried out by small teams of skilled workers often on MSC funding (see 3.3) with additional labour from volunteers. The schemes are jointly funded by the Commission and the local authority, or in the case of the Groundwork Trusts with additional support from private enterprise.

3.2.2 A more specialized countryside management scheme concentrating on small woods is operating on an experimental basis in several counties, e.g., East Sussex, Suffolk. In Scotland a similar scheme, the Central Scotland Woodlands Project, covers the area between Falkirk, Motherwell and Bathgate. These woodland management projects are aimed at conserving small woodlands for timber production, landscape value, amenity and conservation, by providing technical management advice and assistance.

3.2.3   Landowners are recommended to contact their local authority planning department to ascertain if any type of countryside management scheme is being operated in their area, as the project officers will be very willing to assist.

3.3 Manpower Services Commission community programmes

3.3.1   *The MSC Employment Division* runs community programmes involving the long-term unemployed in projects of immediate benefit to the community. On private land such projects must not result in any direct financial gain to the owner, but can include work such as clearing bridle-paths, constructing a trim trail or producing interpretive material. The minimum size of team is three people for a minimum period of three months and maximum of twelve months. Longer periods of work can be accommodated in a rolling programme of tasks for different groups of people.

3.3.2   Landowners interested in the MSC scheme should contact their local Community Programme Manager, via their local Jobcentre.

3.3.3   Details of the scheme are given in the following publication: *The Community Programme*, published by MSC. Source: Jobcentres. Price: Free.

3.4 Military Aid to the Civil Community (MACC)

3.4.1   The MACC scheme may be able to provide specialist assistance on recreation projects, e.g., bridge construction, demolition of dangerous structures, if it is of social value to the community and of training value to the Services. Landowners should contact their Army regional headquarters which is listed below:

HQ Scotland (Army)   For all Scotland
Edinburgh EH1 2YX
Telephone: (031) 336 1761, ext. 6208

HQ North East District   For Northumberland, Tyne &
Fishergate   Wear, Durham, Cleveland,
York YO1 4AU   Yorkshire and Humberside
Telephone: (0904) 59811, ext. 2130

HQ North West District   For Cumbria, Lancashire,
Fulwood Barracks   Manchester, Merseyside and
Preston, Lancashire   Cheshire
Telephone: (0772) 716543, ext. 338

HQ Eastern District   For Derbyshire, Nottinghamshire,
Flagstaff House   Leicestershire, Northamptonshire,
Colchester CO2 7ST   Cambridgeshire, Bedfordshire,
Telephone: (0206) 5121, ext. 2412   Hertfordshire, Essex, Norfolk and
                                        Suffolk

HQ West Midland District   For Staffordshire, West Midlands,
Belle Vue Road   Shropshire, Warwickshire,
Shrewsbury, Shropshire   Herefordshire and Worcestershire
Telephone: (0743) 52234, ext. 241

HQ Wales   For all Wales
The Barracks
Brecon LD3 7EA
Telephone: (0874) 3111, ext. 280

HQ London District   For Greater London
Horseguards
London SW1A 2AX
Telephone: (01) 930 4466, ext. 2444

HQ South East District   For Oxfordshire, Buckingham-
Steeles Road   shire, Berkshire, Hampshire,
Aldershot GU11 2DP   Surrey, Kent and Sussex
Telephone: (0252) 24431, ext. 3191

HQ South West District   For Gloucestershire, Avon, Wilt-
Bulford Camp   shire, Somerset, Devon and
Bulford, Wiltshire SP4 9NY   Cornwall
Telephone: (09803) 3371

Details of the scheme are given in the following publication: *Military Aid to the Civil Community*, published by the Ministry of Defence. Source: Army District HQ. Price: Free.

APPENDIX 4
SOURCES OF FINANCIAL SUPPORT

4.1   Grant aid for capital costs
4.2   Grant aid for recurrent costs
4.3   Grant aid for management and access agreements
4.4   Taxation
4.5   Ticket machines

Note. This area of support alters with the prevailing economic situation and changing government policies, so the sources and levels of help outlined below are liable to vary.

4.1 Grant aid for capital costs

Grant aid towards capital costs may be available for approval projects from the following organizations:

4.1.1   *The Countryside Commission* may grant aid projects up to 50% of the approved costs, although a grant of 30—40% is more usual. Landowners should approach their regional office of Country Commission as given below:

Northern: Warwick House, Grantham Road, Newcastle upon Tyne NE2 1QF. Telephone: (0632) 328353 (for Northumberland, Cumbria, Durham, Tyne & Wear, Cleveland).

North West: 184 Deansgate, Manchester M3 3WB. Telephone: (061) 833 0316 (for Lancashire, Cheshire, Merseyside, Greater Manchester and the Peak District.

Midlands: Cumberland House, 200 Broad Street, Birmingham B15 1TD. Telephone: (021) 632 6503/4 (for Shropshire, Staffordshire, Hereford and Worcester, West Midlands, Warwickshire, Derbyshire except the Peak District, Nottinghamshire, Leicestershire, Northamptonshire).

Office for Wales: 8 Broad Street, Newtown, Powys SY16 2LU. Telephone: (0686) 26799 (for all Wales).

South West: Bridge House, Sion Place, Clifton Down, Bristol BS8 4AS. Telephone: (0272) 739966 (for Gloucestershire, Avon, Wiltshire, Somerset, Dorset, Devon, Cornwall).

Greater London and South East: 30–32 Southampton Street, London WC2E 7RA. Telephone: (01) 240 2771 (for Greater London, Kent, Surrey, Berkshire, Buckinghamshire, Essex, Hertfordshire, Oxfordshire, Sussex, Hampshire, Isle of Wight).

Yorkshire and Humberside: 8A Otley Road, Headingley, Leeds LS6 2AD. Telephone: (0532) 742935/6 (for all Yorkshire, Humberside).

Eastern: Terrington House, 13/15 Hills Road, Cambridge CB2 1NL. Telephone: (0223) 354462 (for Norfolk, Suffolk, Cambridgeshire, Bedfordshire, Lincolnshire).

Publications: *Grants for Recreation Footpaths in the Countryside* CCP 100. *Bridleways and Recreation Policy Statement and Grants* CCP 133. Source: see Appendix 1.1.5. Price: Free.

4.1.2   *The Countryside Commission for Scotland* may offer grants on the cost of approved projects falling within designated countryside. Landowners in Scotland should approach the Commission at the following address: The Countryside Commission for Scotland, Battleby, Redgorton, Perth PH1 3EW. Telephone: (0738) 27921.

Publications: *Countryside Grants to Voluntary Bodies, Community Councils and Individuals*, and *Countryside Grants to Private and Voluntary Bodies and Public Bodies other than Local Authorities*. Source: CCS as above. Price: Free.

4.1.3   *The Sports Council* is mainly concerned with formal sports but may grant aid informal activities up to 50% of the approved costs for items such as a trim trail, path improvements for jogging, bridleway improvements, etc. Landowners in England and Wales should approach their regional Sports Council at the address given in the following leaflet:

Publication: *Finance for Sports Facilities, Grants for Statutory Bodies and Commercial Organisations*. Source: The Publications Unit, The Sports Council, 16 Upper Woburn Place, London WC1H 0QP. Telephone: (01) 388 1277. Price: Free.

4.1.4   *The Scottish Sports Council* does not grant aid informal facilities and landowners in Scotland should approach the Countryside Commission for Scotland (see 4.1.2).

4.1.5   *The Tourist Boards* may grant aid new works or improvement for schemes with tourist potential, e.g., a nature tràil. Landowners should approach their regional tourist boards via the address given in Appendix 1.1.14. The English Tourist Board produces the following useful guides:

Publications: *Financing Tourist Projects* Price £5.00; *How to Approach a Bank for Finance* Price: £1.50; *Services of the Clearing Banks for Developers in Tourism* Price: £1.50; *The Give and Take of Sponsorship* Price: £3.00 Source: see Appendix 1.1.14.

4.1.6   *The Centre for Environmental Interpretation* can advise on possible sources of grant aid for educational and interpretive projects. Centre for Environmental Interpretation, Manchester Polytechnic, John Dalton Building, Chester Street, Manchester M1 5GD. Telephone: (061) 228 6171.

4.1.7   *The Forestry Commission* does not grant aid recreation projects, but encourages woodland owners receiving forestry grants to consider public access. The FC scheme covers woodland of 0.25 ha and over, and details of the scheme are available from the FC at: The Forestry Commission, 231 Corstorphine Road. Edinburgh EH12 7AT. Telephone: (031) 334 0303.

Publication: *Forestry Grant Scheme*. Source: FC (as above). Price: Free.

Note. Woodlands of under 0.25 ha may be eligible for grant aid towards the costs of management from the Countryside Commission.

In most areas grant schemes are run for the Countryside Commission by County Councils and applications should be sent to the County Forestry Officer.

Publication: *Conservation Grants for Farmers and Landowners* CCP 171. Source: CC (see Appendix 1.1.5). Price: Free.

Note. The FC is considering a new grant scheme for broadleaved woodland that may be of interest to urban-fringe landowners.

Publication: *Broadleaves in Britain. A Consultative Paper*. Source: as above. Price: £3.00.

4.1.8   *Development Agencies may be interested* in assisting urban-fringe schemes where there is likely to be some community benefit in terms of employment or visitor expenditure. Landowners should approach the relevant organization for their area, e.g.: The Welsh Development Agency, The Scottish Development Agency, The Highlands and Islands Development Board.

4.2 Grant aid for recurrent costs

Grant aid towards recurrent costs is unlikely except for new ideas which government and others wish to encourage.

4.2.1   *The Countryside Commission* grant aids some ranger services although it is unlikely that a service provided by a landowner on a single site would be eligible for grant. Landowners should approach their regional office of the Countryside Commission (see 4.1.1).

Note. The CC also sponsor training courses for newly-appointed rangers; contact the CC regional office for details.

Publication: *Countryside Rangers and Related Staff*, Advisory Series No. 7. Source: Countryside Commission (see 1.1.5). Price: Free.

4.2.2   *The Countryside Commission for Scotland* may offer grants on ranger services in designated countryside at the rate of up to 75%. Grant aid may also be available for capital items related to the ranger service, e.g., vehicles, walkie-talkies, binoculars, etc. Landowners in Scotland should approach the Commission at the address given in Appendix 4.1.2.

Publications: *Countryside Rangers in Scotland*, and *Grants for Countryside Ranger Services*. Source: CCS (see 4.1.2). Price: Free.

4.2.3   *The Centre for Environmental Interpretation* can advise on the possible sources of grant aid for recurrent costs at educational or interpretive projects, see 4.1.6.

4.3 Grant aid for management and access agreements

4.3.1   *The Countryside Commission* will grant aid management agreements between local authorities and private landowners up to 75% of approved expenditure in Areas of Outstanding Natural Beauty and up to 50% in other areas. Improved public access, recreational management and sites in country-side management schemes will be favoured and agreements should run for a period of years.

The Commission is also able to grant aid access agreements between local authorities and landowners, normally in the form of an annual payment. Such agreements include provision for access to be restricted in certain circum-stances, e.g., exceptional fire risk, and for the local authority to provide wardens. Landowners should approach their regional office of the Com-mission (see 4.1.1).

Publications: *Management Agreements, Policy Statements and Grants* CCP 156. Source: CC (see Appendix 1.1.5). Price: Free. *Wildlife and Countryside Act 1981. Financial Guidelines for Management Agreements*. Source: HMSO. Price: £2.45.

4.3.2   *The Countryside Commission for Scotland* may also help defray expenditure arising from management agreements. Landowners should approach the Commission at the address given in Appendix 4.1.2.

Publications: *Access Agreements. Management Agreements*. Source: CCS (see Appendix 4.1.2). Price: Free.

4.4 Taxation

4.4.1   The current Inland Revenue and Forestry Commission publications do not give specific advice about recreation expenditure or revenue in woodlands, and unfortunately it is not the policy of the Inland Revenue Technical Division to comment on hypothetical situations. As cases depend on the particular facts of an individual's circumstances, landowners are recommended to seek professional advice as to the style of development most appropriate to their circumstances.

4.4.2   However, landowners' attention is drawn to the possibilities of claiming tax relief for expenditure on recreational items in the following circumstances:

Rents, wayleaves or sporting right which provide income taxed under Schedule A. Allowances against tax include expenditure on maintenance, repair, insurance, management and other *non-capital items*.

Trading with a view of realizing a profit, either recreational enterprises or under the option to have commercial woodlands assessed for trading profits under Schedule D Case 1. Allowances against tax include *expenditure on capital items*, machinery and plant and operating costs, net of any grants received.

Other annual income such as from non-commercial operations, e.g., parking charges, entry fees, assessed under Schedule D Case VI. Allowances against tax include only recurrent items, not capital items such as the car park itself.

4.4.3   Landowners should note that tax relief on recreational expenditure can only be claimed in circumstances which generate, or are intended to generate an income. In other words, where such expenditure is purely philanthropic and there is no taxable income it is not eligible for tax relief.

Schedule A: Tax on rents and other periodic payments from property

4.4.4   In the context of recreation, this covers income from sources such as rent for a campsite used by a club; income from wayleaves for horse riding; income from a shooting syndicate.

Landowners should note that chalets and cabins let for holidays without creating a tenancy are not taxed under Schedule A, but as trading income, Schedule D Case I.

4.4.5   Allowances against tax are for the expenses of the transaction and could include the following non-capital items (but landowners should note that an exception to the non-capital rule is made for plant and machinery required to maintain the property):

Maintenance of wayleaves, rides, roads, etc., particularly important in relation to horse-riding impact.

The cost of plant and machinery used to maintain or repair the property, e.g., a mower for a campsite, or a dozer-blade for the tractor for ride repair.

Salaries or wages of staff engaged full time on estate management, e.g., keeper

of a shooting syndicate.
Premium on policies to insure the property against the risk of damage by fire.

4.4.6   Landowners should note that where the income, such as sporting rental is being generated in a Schedule B woodland, Schedule A tax is only charged on that amount by which the sporting income exceeds the Schedule B assessable value.

4.4.7   Where expenditure exceeds income in a tax year, the excess may be charged against income from similar sources, e.g., another wayleave or shoot, or carried forward to the following tax year.

4.4.8   An explanation of Schedule A tax and the items for which tax relief is given, is contained in the following publications:

Notes on the Taxation of Income from Real Property Booklet IR27. Published by the Inland Revenue. Source: Local Tax Office. Price: Free.

Butterworth's UK Tax Guide, 1984–1985, Chapter 9 (revised annually). Published by Butterworth's. Source: Bookshops. Price: £12.00.

Schedule D Case I: Tax on trading profits

4.4.9   Where a landowner has chosen to have a woodland taxed under Schedule D on its trading profits, recreation expenditure to protect the woodland from unmanaged access should be included in the forestry account.

4.4.10   Unlike Schedule A, *capital and maintenance allowances* are granted under Schedule D, and also any excess expenditure over income in any year may be offset against the owner's *income from other sources*. This is of particular interest to owners paying income tax at higher rates. Alternatively, the tax relief may be carried forward to be held against future income in the forestry account. Any income from recreation should also go through the forestry account except for rental and other periodic payments assessed under Schedule A.

4.4.11   Schedule D Case I would also apply to a landowner who was operating a recreational enterprise with a view to realizing a profit, where this is not part of a commercial forestry venture, for example in an amenity woodland. The tax relief on capital and maintenance expenditure would be allowed and any excess carried forward or offset against income from other sources.

4.4.12   Without giving specific advice about woodland recreation, the following publications give details of Schedule D taxation:

Taxation of Woodlands Forestry Commission Leaflet 12. Source: HMSO. Price: £1.00.

Capital Allowances of Machinery or Plant (New System) Board of Inland Revenue Leaflet CA1. Source: Local Tax Office. Price: Free.

Capital Allowances on Agricultural or Forestry Buildings or Works Inland Revenue Leaflet CA3. Source: Local Tax Office. Price: Free.

Butterworth's UK Tax Guide 1984—1985, Chapters 7 and 8. Published by Butterworth's. Source: Bookshops. Price: £12.00.

Schedule D Case VI: Tax on other income

4.4.13   This case catches income from residual sources which in the context of woodland recreation would include income from non-commercial ventures, i.e., those not being operated with a view to realizing a profit, or not part of a commercial woodland enterprise. Examples could include revenue from parking fees; revenue from guided walks round the woodland.

4.4.14   Allowances are less advantageous as they exclude items of capital expenditure and only cover the landowner's operating costs of collecting the income. Any excess relief can only be held against income from a similar source or rolled forward. Further information is given in the following publication:

Butterworth's UK Tax Guide 1984—1985, Chapter 10. Published by Butterworth's. Source: Bookshops. Price: £12.00.

Schedule B: Taxation of commercial woodlands

4.4.15   Schedule B is the 'normal' tax schedule for older woodlands (unless the owner has chosen to be taxed under Schedule D) and is on the basis of *one third of the annual rental value of land in the unimproved state*. While allowing an owner to take the profits from selling any timber without any additional taxation, there are no allowances for capital or maintenance costs. In the context of woodland recreation, this means, any schemes involving capital works or regular maintenance would not be deductable for tax purposes, as part of the forestry enterprise. Equally, any recreational income which is part of the forestry enterprise may be included in the Schedule B assessment and not liable to tax, but this is a grey area.

4.4.16   Certainly rental income from a Schedule B woodland is still taxable under Schedule A, to the extent that the rental income exceeds the Schedule B valuation. Woodland owners converting timber beyond the planking state have been deemed to be trading and liable for tax under Schedule D Case I. As recreation income is so rare at present, there is no case law which can give landowners guidance, although some claim their Schedule 'B' assessment covers the recreation income from the forestry enterprise.

4.4.17   If recreational income is not covered by the Schedule B assessment, owners may need to consider operating a recreational enterprise "with a view to realizing a profit", for assessment under Schedule D Case I, rather than a non-profit-making enterprise which would be caught under Case VI with its less generous allowances.

4.4.18   This whole area of taxation of woodland recreation is not clear at present and the recommendation to seek professional advice is reiterated. Table 4.4.1 below attempts to summarize the position. Where commercial woodlands are occupied by companies, the tax options of Schedules B or D still apply, but landowners should assess the advantages and disadvantages of establishing a recreation company (see 4.4.19).

Table 4.4.1 — Taxation schedules and woodland recreation

Recreational use	Amenity wood	Schedule B wood	Schedule D wood
Rents, wayleaves and sporting rights	Income assessed under Schedule A	Excess income over Schedule B valuation assessed under Schedule A	Income assessed under Schedule A
	Allowances for maintenance, repairs, insurance, management and other non-capital expenditure, under Schedule A		
Holiday lettings	Income assessed under Schedule D Case I 'trading profits'		
	Allowances for capital and operating costs		
Commercial recreation	Income assessed under Schedule D Case I Allowances on capital and operating costs	Possibly part of forestry enterprise and included in Schedule B; Otherwise Schedule D Case I No allowances under Schedule B, but capital and operating costs allowed under Schedule D Case I	Part of forestry enterprise and included in accounts for Schedule D Case I; Allowances on capital and operating costs
Non-commercial recreation	Income assessed under Schedule D Case VI; Allowances on operating costs and non-capital expenditure	Possibly part of the forestry enterprise and included in Schedule B; Otherwise Schedule D Case VI	Part of forestry enterprise and included in accounts for Schedule D Case I; Allowances on capital and operating costs

4.4.19   The English Tourist Board (ETB) have produced a series of publications of more general interest which may be relevant to woodland recreation in certain situations.

Publications: *Development Land Tax*; *Capital Transfer Tax*; *Taxation of Hotels and other Leisure Enterprises*; *When to Form a Limited Company*. Source: ETB (see 1.1.14). Price: £1.50 each.

4.5 Ticket machines

4.5.1   The Forestry Commission and National Trust use simple mechanical machines which produce serial-numbered but undated tickets, and operate on 10p, 20p or 50p coins. The machines are best installed in a wall or pillar, particularly where vandalism and petty crime is a problem. The machines can be rented from the manufacturer for *c.* £100 p.a., including maintenance (1984 price) and are called the 'SMS Stamper'.

Manufacturer: Hillday Limited, 1A Haverscroft Industrial Estate, Attleborough, Norfolk. Telephone: (0953) 454014.

APPENDIX 5
SOURCES OF ADVICE ON CONSERVATION

5.1   Advisory services
5.2   Publications

5.1 Advisory services

Landowners seeking advice about nature conservation in their woodland, its importance, management techniques and general advice, should approach the following bodies:

5.1.1   *The Nature Conservancy Council* (NCC), Northminster House, Peterborough PE1 1UA. Telephone: (0733) 40345.

5.1.2   *The Royal Society for Nature Conservation* (RSNC), The Green, Nettleham, Lincoln LN2 2NR. Telephone: (0522) 752326.

The RSNC will advise landowners of their local County Trust for Nature Conservation, who will be very willing to help.

5.1.3   *The Royal Society for the Protection of Birds* (RSPB), The Lodge, Sandy, Bedfordshire SG19 2DL. Telephone (0767) 80551.

The RSPB has a limited advisory service for woodland owners; contact John Andrews, Conservation Department.

5.2 Publications

5.2.1   *The Conservation of lowland broadleaf woodland.* Publisher: NCC. Source: NCC (see 5.1.1). Price: £0.30.

5.2.2   *The Conservation of semi-natural upland woodland.* Publisher: NCC. Source: NCC (see 5.1.1). Price: £0.30.

5.2.3   *Tree Planting.* Published by NCC. Source: NCC (see 5.1.1). Price: £0.20.

5.2.4   *Hedges and Shelter Belts.* Published by NCC. Source: NCC (see 5.1.1).

5.2.5   General Management Principles for Nature Conservation in British Woodlands by G F Peterken (1977). In: *Forestry* Vol. 50, No. 1, pages 27—48. Source: Libraries.
A further account of the principles and the rationale behind them is contained in 5.2.6.

5.2.6   *Woodland Management and Conservation* by G F Peterken. Published by Chapman and Hall (1981). Source: Bookshops. Price: £25.

5.2.7.   *Wildlife Conservation in Woodlands* by R C Steele. Published by Forestry Commission, Booklet 29. Source: HMSO. Price: £0.75.

5.2.8   *Silviculture of Broadleaved Woodland* by Dr J Evans. Published by Forestry Commission, Bulletin 62. Source: HMSO. Price: £9.50.

5.2.9   *The Management of Semi-Natural Woodland*. Published by Hampshire County Council. Source: HCC, The Castle, Winchester. Price: £2.00.

5.2.10   *Birds and Woodland Handbook*. Published by RSPB (in preparation). Source: RSPB (see 5.1.3). Price: to be announced.

REFERENCES

[1]   Collins, M F. The growing need for access to the countryside and its responsible enjoyment. In *Public Access and Countryside Sports*, 12th Meeting of the Standing Conference on Countryside Sports, 23 November 1983, SSCS, College of Estate Management, Reading.

[2]   Mattingly, A. Report of a talk to the London Wildlife Trust, reported in *Planning*, 22.6.84.

[3]   Royston, K. Private Estates and public relations, *Chartered Surveyor Weekly* 5(11) 684—685; 1983.

[4]   Country Landowners' Association. *Landowners and the Countryside — 2 Agreeing on Access*, CLA, London, 1984.

[5]   Tartaglia-Kershaw, M. The recreational and aesthetic significance of urban woodland. *Landscape Research* 7(3) 22—25; 1982.

[6]   Tourism & Recreation Research Unit. *Pollok Park 1979: A visitor survey and Review of Management Implications*. TRRU Research Report No. 45, Edinburgh University, 1980.

[7]   Tourism & Recreation Research Unit. *The Woodland Visitor*. TRRU Research Report No. 20, Edinburgh University, 1978.

[8]   Goodall, B & Whittow, J B. *Recreation Requirements and Forest Opportunities*, Geographical Papers No. 37, University of Reading, 1975.

[9]   Forestry Commission. *Forestry Practice* (Ch. 7, Recreation). FC Bulletin 14, HMSO, London, 1978.

[10]   Tourism & Recreation Research Unit. *A Study of four parks in and*

around Glasgow. TRRU Research Report No. 44, Edinburgh University, 1980.

[11] Harrison, C M. Countryside Recreation and London's Urban Fringe. *Transactions of the Institute of British Geographers*, NS8: 295–313, 1983.

[12] Milton Keynes Development Corporation. *Linford Wood Visitors Survey.* Recreation Study 1. Recreation Unit, MKDC, 1980.

[13] Milton Keynes Development Corporation. *Linford Wood User Survey* in *Industrial Placement Report 1981–82* by Colin Williams, Appendix 2, Recreation Unit MKDC, 1982.

[14] Ramblers' Association. *Open Country: Public Asset or Private Domain?* RA Brief for the Countryside No. 9, Ramblers' Association, London, 1982.

[15] Cooke, A S. Observation on how close certain passerine species will tolerate an approaching human in rural and suburban areas. *Biological Conservation* 18 85–88, 1980.

[16] Prior, R. The effect of Disturbance on Deer in *Public Access and Countryside Sports*, 12th Meeting of the Standing Conference on Countryside Sports 23 November 1983, SCCS, College of Estate Management, Reading, 1983.

[17] Crowe, S. *The Landscape of Forests and Woods*, Forestry Commission Booklet No. 44, HMSO, London, 1978.

[18] Kassioumis, C. *Recreationists' response to Forests and the Implication for Forestry and Recreation Management.* Geographical Papers No. 74, University of Reading, 1981.

NOTES